Colonial Massachusetts, 1650-1781

James Biser Whisker

John R. Coe

Copyright by James Biser Whisker
All rights reserved.
Printed and distributed in
the United States of America
by KDP./Amazon

John R Coe was born and raised in Parkersburg, WV. He was the youngest child of the late Dr. Donald E. Coe and Jacqueline Ann Galka. He received his B.S. degree in biology from Glenville State College, his MS from WVU, and his Ed. D. from Liberty University. He is also a retired central office administrator from the Wood County schools. John is currently an independent businessman . The businesses include an analytical chemistry lab as well as a restaurant. He is an avid firearm collector of both pistols rifles and muzzle loaders. He can be found almost any day on the rifle range. He has been married for over 31 years to his college sweetheart Rosemary. In October 2023 he received Doctor Humane Letters from the Society of Fellows of Edwin Mellen University.

James B Whisker is professor emeritus from West Virginia University where he taught for over 37 years. He was adviser to the WVU College Republicans during most of his tenure. He received his B.S. From Mount St. Mary's College and M.A. degrees in philosophy and history from Niagara University, and his Ph. D. in 1969 from the University of Maryland. He is author or co-author of books on gunsmiths and arms makers of eighteen states. Among his other books are *The Alien Tort Claims Act, The Militia, The Right to Hunt; The Citizen-Soldier and U.S. Military Policy, Our Vanishing Freedom: The Right to Keep and Bear Arms; Nihilism: The Philosophy of Nothingness; Asylum and Sanctuary in History and Law; The Just War Doctrine in Catholic Thought; Capital Punishment in Religious and Political Thought;* and the *Rise and Decline of the American Militia System.* In October 2023 he received Doctor Humane Letters from the Society of Fellows of Edwin Mellen University. He currently resides in Everett. In August 2023 he and, the former Sheila Elaine Bailey celebrated their 53rd wedding anniversary. The couple has two sons and four grandchildren.

Contents

Introduction..7
The Political Pulpit..25
The Colonial Militia..41
King Philip's War...70
The Massachusetts Militia in the Early 18th Century..................86
The Seven Years War..102
The Militia in the Revolution....................................121
Militia Law during the Revolution...........................141
Appendix: Dodge fowling piece................................157
Bibliography..161

This book is respectfully dedicated to

Jacques Ralph Andrè Williams, Esquire

Attorney, Humanitarian, Scholar, Friend

Introduction

When the Puritans landed in New England they wished to found their own city on the hill, secular paradise, or land of the chosen people. Initially, the Pilgrims courted the indigenous Amerindians and became friends with the Wampanoags. The Massachusetts colony was wholly separatist and wanted nothing more than to be left alone. In the earliest years there was virtually no need for a strong military system. The friendship was short-lived, for the Europeans never did quite master the skill of being good neighbors to the Amerindians and leaving them alone. Within ten years the Puritans had come to regard themselves as the new Zion and the Amerindians as Canaanites. They did not regard themselves as interlopers, but as God's chosen people for whom the new land had been prepared, and which they could develop without limitation. Like the Jews of the Exodus, the Puritans did not spare the Canaanites. Within ten years after the Puritans initially landed those at Boston had formed a mighty militia system.

The Puritan colonists decided to create a covenanted militia which they effected within a few years after they had originally settled. They especially decided to avoid creating a professional officer class. They avowed to not copy the militia system which they had known in England. Rather, they created a new kind of militia which allowed for the free election of officers. As early as 1632, Governor Winthrop reported, "A proposition was made by the people, that every company of trained men might choose their own captain and officers."[1] Puritan leaders had logically concluded that the same men who had elected representatives and ministers should also be the ones to choose military commanders. However, as one Puritan writer noted, "There are none chosen to office in any of these Bands, but such as are freemen supposed to be men indued with faith in Christ Jesus."[2]

Three separate, and often mutually distrustful, authorities vied for control of the New England militias. First, each colony had its own militia organization which was identical with, or responsible to, the colonial legislature and/or governor. Second, the New England colonies having created a unified military plan known as the New

---

1   Winthrop, John. *History of New England.* James K. Hosmer, ed. 2 vols (1908), 1: 79.
2   Johnson, Edward. *The Wonder-Working Providence of Sions Savior in New England.* J. F. Jameson, ed. (1910), p. 231

England Confederation, placed their individual militias under this regional authority. At various times the individual colonial authorities refused to cooperate and release militiamen to assist the general authority. Massachusetts refused to assist the other members in the first Narragansett War (1645-50) when it was not especially threatened, but demanded assistance from the other colonies when in 1675 in the second Narragansett War it was sacked and pillaged.

Third, the mother country was the ultimate sovereign authority that periodically intervened in local militia affairs. As with most other aspects of colonial policy, England generally neglected the colonies, but on occasion it attempted to impose its will on its dependencies. The colonial militias usually provided for virtually all of their own colonies' defense and this freed the English standing army for larger and, to the mother nation, more important duties. In general, the colonies were delighted to receive money, materials, equipment, and arms from England, but they disliked the brutal discipline and elitist attitude of the professional officer corps and they held the army in disdain for it was essentially useless in frontier warfare against savages who did not follow the rules of European warfare. They especially resented English intrusion into the appointment of militia officers.[3]

Future President John Adams asserted that there were four institutions of importance in colonial Massachusetts: towns, schools, religious congregations, and the militia. Each of these fundamental associations was thoroughly integrated with the other three. Each changed as the colony matured. As the threat of Amerindian and French attacks was removed the militia became ever more a fraternal association. Each of these, in its own way, contributed to the American War for Independence. They were also the cornerstones of liberty, happiness, and prosperity. If only because there were no formal police departments, the New England colonies merged the militia with the night watch. The Massachusetts system of defense reveals that it was as much an expression of Puritan social ideas as were the New England town meetings and the Congregational churches. Indeed, the history of the village trainbands paralleled the development of other, more obviously Puritan institutions.[4]

---

3   Breen, T. H., "English Origins and New World Development: The Case of the Covenanted Militia in Seventeenth Century Massachusetts," *Past and Present,* 58 (1972), pp. 3-25.
4   Adams, John. *The Works of John Adams.* Charles F. Adams, ed. Boston, 1851, 5: 494-5.

Militia organization, according to John Adams writing as as *Novanglus,* removed the "men who procured their commissions from a governor as reward for making themselves pimps to his tools." In their place stood the natural elite of a free people: "gentlemen whose estates, abilities, and benevolence, have rendered them the delight of the soldiers." The reorganized militia represented not only a military organization designed to stem British oppression, but also a constitutional order historically linked with the preservation of civil liberties and personal freedom.[5]

From the very beginning, the colonial militia system was grounded in the principle of universal obligation. All the colonial militias, except Pennsylvania which had none, enrolled every able-bodied male between (usually) the ages of sixteen and sixty. Citizens were required to furnish their own arms and accouterments. Heads of household had to furnish these items for all eligible males under their supervision. Once equipped, they to muster for regularly scheduled training, and the failure to do so was punished by fines. This mandatory training could be held as frequently as once a week or be reduced to only a few musters per year. The colonial militia system was clearly an early version of universal military training.

There was a second coercive element which came into play only when the militia was called to gather for active military service. The entire militia was rarely mustered, and then only for great emergencies, and only for a short period of time. In such cases as when a government undertook a military campaign, it would set quotas for to be filled by various local militia organizations, commonly based upon the number of eligibiles.[6] The local militias would attempt to fill the quotas with volunteers, but not infrequently they would have to offer bounties, involving money, land, and equipment. Many impoverished youths chose military service as a means to support and perhaps even saving a bit of money. If the quotas were still unfilled, they would resort to using drafts. In some, but not all, cases one might avoid being drafted were by either paying a fine or hiring a substitute. Colonial governments made frequent use of militia drafts during the Amerindian wars and their wars against France and Spain. On rare occasion,

---

5 "Novanglus, No. 3", in Bernard Mason, ed., *The American Colonial Crisis: The Daniel Leonard-John Adams Letters to the Press, 1774-1775.* Harper and Row, 1972, p. 131.

6 O'Sullivan, John; and Alan M. Meckler. *The Draft and Its Enemies: A Documentary History,* University of Illinois Press, 1974, p. 5,

colonial governments directly impressed men. They preferred to follow the English practice, choosing men from among the lower strata of society, rather than drafting from militia rolls. Jails, alms houses, and poverty rows served well for such recruitment.[7]

In addition to the legally constituted militia, in most colonies there existed volunteer militia units, which were privately recruited. Among the earliest volunteer units was the Ancient and Honorable Artillery Company of Boston, organized in 1636. Initially, these volunteer units operated independent of the colonial militias. Later, colonial governments found it useful to integrate them into the general militia systems, giving them full legal status. Volunteer militia units provided much of the cavalry and artillery, along with certain elite infantry available during the early periods. The volunteers bore the expense of their own horses in cavalry and often of their company's cannon nad gunpowder for artillery. Men could gain exemption from the common militia by joining a volunteer unit.[8]

The New England Puritans of c.1630 were displeased with the English militia system for a variety of reasons. King Charles I had reorganized the English militia, creating a far more elitist and disciplined organization than his father, James I, had possessed. He brought veteran professional military men, many the veterans of several continental European wars, to train and discipline the raw militia recruits. He also introduced new weapons and required that existing weapons, most long neglected and in a sad state of disrepair, be properly mended. He angered the Puritans by requiring that, following church services on Sundays, the train bands were to engage in such sports as "archery, running, wrestling, leaping, football playing, casting the sledge hammer and playing at cudgels."[9] The Puritans regarded these activities as the manifestation of sacrilegious violations of

---

[7] The English origins the American militia recruitment system is well covered in Michael Powicke, *Military Obligation in Medieval England: A Study in Liberty and Duty.* Oxford: at the Clarendon Press, 1962. See also J.R. Western, *The English Militia in the Eighteenth Century: The Story of a Political Issue, 1660–1802.* Routledge & Kegan Paul, 1965.

[8] Mahon, John K. *The American Militia: Decade of Decision, 1789–1800.* University of Florida Press, 1960, pp. 56–61. Mahon used the term "special militia" to differentiate between independent units formally outside the militia system, and volunteer units formally within it.

[9] This objection to excess militarism on Sundays was repeated in the 1760s. This time it was the practice of the British army stationed at Boston that upset the citizenry. *New York Journal, Supplement,* 13 and 20 July 1769.

the Sabbath which they argued was to be a day of rest and not of praying and playing games. Thus, Charles added a religious question to the existing legal and constitutional questions concerning his reorganization of the militia. For his part, Charles bragged that his reorganized train band system was "the perfect militia."[10]

The English Puritan brethren had rejected the militia policies of Charles I and in the bitter debate in the parliamentary session of 1628 railed hard against the imposition of tyrannical standards on an essentially civilian body.[11] Those Puritans who sailed with John Winthrop in 1630 had an idea of a militia constituted in a way quite different from the Stuart train bands. There was no question that they would create a militia, for they were well aware of the massacre of the ill-prepared Virginians at the hands of the Indians in 1622. But the Pilgrim fathers did not agree with Charles I that his idea of a train band was a perfect militia.[12]

The Charter of New England of 1620 created a militia primarily as an instrument to contain "Rebellion, Insurrection and Mutiny" against the crown. The militia was also to "encounter, expulse, repel and resist by Force of Arms" by "all ways and meanes" whatever foreign or native forces might be directed against the colony. The charter made the president the militia commander, although the assent of council was needed to deploy the militia. Council was to make appropriate laws for enrollment, training and discipline of the militia. The charter required the president and council to supply arms, ammunition and other goods of war.[13]

The New England Puritans first hired professional military men to equip, drill and train the militia, but these men were veteran soldiers who were not Puritans and did not share the religious vision of the city on the hill. They had a particular dislike for the demand the Puritan made that they be allowed to elect officers, an idea inconceivable to professional military men. They were also expensive,

---

10 Boynton, Lindsay. *The Elizabethan Militia, 1558-1638*. Routledge and K. Paul, 1967, pp. 246-50.
11 Boynton, *Elizabethan Militia*, pp. 275-93.
12 Shy, John. *Toward Lexington*. Princeton University Press, 1965; Darrell Rutman, "A Militant New World, 1607-1640." University of Virginia Ph. D. dissertation, 1959.
13 Poore, Benjamin P., ed. *The Federal and State Constitutions, Colonial Charters and Other Organic Laws of the United States*. 2 vols. U. S. Government Printing Office, 1877, 1: 925-29.

both in terms of pay and in terms of the discontent they fostered in the colony. Jost Weillust, a German artillery specialist, left the Massachusetts Bay Colony almost immediately, not having acquired any love for the new land, but also perhaps overcome by homesickness. Daniel Patrick and John Underhill lasted somewhat longer, but they never became comfortable with the spartan life of New England Puritanism. Both were accused of having committed adultery with young women of the community and were asked to leave. Underhill was a true military professional, and was greatly annoyed when the Salem militia put the ordinance into effect, appointing in Underhill's words "a Captaine, Lieutenant, and Ensigne . . . after such a manner as never was heard of in any Schoole of warre; nor in no Kingedome under heaven." He immediately wrote to the Governor, warning, "For my parte, if there should not be a reformation in this disordered practise, I would not acknowledge such Officers."[14] Eventually, Underhill and the Puritans parted company on less than friendly terms. He observed with disgust that the Puritans were, at best, "soldiers not accustomed to war" who were "unexpert in the use of their arms."[15] The political authorities of New England decided that henceforth they would hire only Puritans, whether they were military veterans or not.

There were many demands for money to fund various governmental activities and the tax base was small. One of the larger items in the defense budgets was the erection and maintenance of frontier fortifications. To save money the militias were originally all volunteer organizations. Many militiamen objected to their deployment in construction and maintenance of forts and places of refuge. However, when the governments failed to recruit enough volunteers to complete the work, they turned to the draft to fill out the quota of volunteer workmen. The draft depleted the resources of many militia companies.[16]

---

14 Quoted in John Winthrop. *Winthrop Papers.* 5 vols. Massachusetts Historical Society, 1929-47, 3: 503-04.

15 Roberts, Oliver A. *History of the . . . Ancient and Honorable Artillery Company of Massachusetts, 1637-1888.* Boston: Mudge, 1895, 1: 1-3; L. E. DeForest. *Captain John Underhill: Gentleman, Soldier of Fortune.* New York: Underhill Society of America, 1934, pp. 6-7, 28; John Winthrop. *History of New England.* J. K. Hosmer, ed. New York: Holt, 1908, I: 78; 2: 153-54.

16 *Records of the Governor and Company of Massachusetts Bay in New England.* Nathaniel B. Shurtleff, ed. 5 vols. State of Massachusetts, 1854. 2: 222; 4, part 2: 575; 5: 48, 71, 76, 123, 144-45. See also *The Compact with the Charters and Laws of the Colony of New Plymouth.* William Brigham, ed. State of Massachu-

Beginning with the Mayflower Compact of 11 November 1620 the New England colony had been founded upon a social contract. The colonists believed that the only way free men could be brought to obey the law was to base the law upon a contract upon which all agreed. The New England Puritans had a strong sense of democracy and they demanded broad based political participation in all decision making. The social contract had a natural law, Scriptural base. Each man agreed to give up his own interest and benefits voluntarily to the greater community in exchange for protection and congeniality. Among free men no amount of coercion could replace voluntary consent of the governed as the cornerstone of the polity. The congregational churches, election of ministers and magistrates, creation of state and town governments, and organization of the militia were all arranged contractually. Thomas Hooker (1586-1647), one of the most important of the Puritan theorists, argued that a man who desired to live a good life in a Christian polity must "willingly binde and ingage himself to each member of that society . . . or else a member actually he is not."[17] Each man under contract viewed himself as the author of law and the creator of order.

This contractual model extended to the founding and operation of the militia. The major application of the contractual principle extended to recruiting and training a militia in New England and with the popular election of militia officers. The New England militia was a contractual or covenanted organization, based on the principle of voluntary collectivism. A contractual militia was no threat to civil liberties, freedom or civil rights, especially when tied to Scripture. The contract limited deployment of troops and militiamen argued that no governmental power could force them to serve beyond the boundaries of their own colony, and only rarely beyond their own region.[18]

In times of trials and external threats the Puritans frequently called for fasting among the entire community as a means of supporting their militiamen. Fasting served as communal expiation for their un-Christian divisiveness within the ranks of the faithful. It also

---

setts, 1836. *Records of the Colony of New Plymouth in New England.* Nathaniel Shurtleff, ed. 10: 360. Hereinafter cited as *Plymouth Col. Rec.*
17 Hooker, Thomas. *A Survey of the Summe of Church Disciple.* London: Bellamy, 1648, I: 47.
18 *The Colonial Laws of Massachusetts reprinted from the Edition of 1660, with Supplements to 1672, Containing also the Body of Liberties of 1641.* W. H. Whitmore, ed. Boston: State of Massachusetts, c.1860, p. 35.

served to assist in communal re-dedication to their sacred covenant.[19] As late as the 1760s, while Boston was under the yoke of British occupation forces who were being quartered in private homes, Governor Bernard called for "a general fast, to be kept the sixth of April next" offered up so that "God would be graciously pleased to continue us, the enjoyment of all our invaluable privileges, of a civil and religious nature."[20]

The British authorities intensely disliked this democratic practice. When Sir Charles Hardy in 1756 was raising troops for his attack on the French fort at Crown Point he complained bitterly about the practice of the militiamen electing their own officers.

> Pray, my Lord, where have these men come from? Under the vote for raising the Men . . . the Men have it in their own Choice & are supported in it by a law of the Colony from whence they came, and the Consequence is plain . . . . The present Method is attendant with great Delays . . . . Captains of the Regulars will think it hard to be commanded by Field Officers of the Provincials & the Field Officers will likewise think so in having them on equal foot . . . . All Men raised in the Provinces for his Majesty's Service should be raised by the Commander in Chief who may give blank Commissions in such Numbers he thinks proper, to the several Governors, to fill up with the Names of such Persons as may be qualified . . . .[21]

In the other colonies the officers were appointed by the governors, proprietors or legislature. In practice it made little difference because the New Englanders were generally much persuaded to recruit officers from among the better class, which frequently translated to the religious hierarchy. There was no discernible difference between the military and the social structure of the community.

As early as 1632 Governor Winthrop noted that the people had demanded the right of free men to select their own officers.[22] He was able to delay the grant of this right temporarily, for the Puritans had long since decided that free men who could elect their own ministers and political leaders could certainly be entrusted with the selection of

---

19 Hall, David D. *Worlds of Wonder, Days of Judgment: Popular Religious Beliefs in Early New England.* Knopf, 1989, pp. 169-72.
20 *New York Journal,* Supplement, 27 April 1769.
21 Sir Charles Hardy to the Earl of Halifax, dated 7 May 1756, in Stanley Pargellis, editor. *Military Affairs in North America, 1748-1756.* Hampden, Ct.: Anchor, 1969, p. 172.
22 Winthrop, *History of New England,* 1: 79.

militia officers. Besides, it was their very lives, and not the life of the governor, they were entrusting to their elected officers. The legislature took its time, waiting to force the governor's hand at the first opportunity. That opportunity came in 1636 as the colony prepared for war with the Pequot Indians. The Massachusetts General Court enacted legislation allowing each regiment and company to nominate its own officers, subject to ratification by the council. In practice, this confirmation was ordinarily automatic. The militia units responded immediately by holding elections and sending in the names for approval. The requirements for becoming an officer, in addition to election, were correct church membership and status as freemen.[23] In a few cases, the militia units would send up more names than were actually needed, or additional names after council had questioned a name, but frequently these additional names were found to be disqualified on some ground. In 1643 the general court fully yielded its power to appoint militia offices, although it still appointed sergeant major general, the highest office in the New England colonies. However, the company sergeant-majors, were made elective.[24]

As late as the era of the American Revolution the practice of election of officers came under criticism of several experienced military and some legislators from the middle and southern colonies. General George Washington, for example, disliked the practice of electing officers because he believed that it was misplaced democracy, was wholly inappropriate to the martial spirit, and that it subverted attempts to foster military temperament. During the war Washington cashiered several officers because they had fraternized too much with their men. Such fraternal relations, Washington reasoned, would subvert discipline, while doing nothing to create a spirit of command. He argued that the only way to select officers was to test the military prowess and competence and learning in the art of war.[25]

While the English regarded the Puritans as hopelessly democratic, the colony of Massachusetts Bay still had a rigid class structure, seen nowhere better than in its militia organization. The wealthy

---

23 Winthrop, *History of New England*, 1: 125; *Massachusetts Colonial Records*, 1: 187-88; Sharp, "Leadership and Democracy," pp. 256-58; Edward Johnson, *The Wonder Working Providence of Sions Savior in New England* [1654]. J. F. Jameson, ed. Scribner's, 1910, p. 231; Breen, "English Origins,"p. 84.
24 Winthrop, *History of New England,* 3: 503-04; 4: 106; *Massachusetts Colonial Records,* 1: 221, 231
25 Alden, John R. *A History of the American Revolution.* Knopf, 1969, p. 253.

citizens who could afford the equipment organized as cavalry, which became the elite units within the militia. The underclass, on the other hand, supplied the foot soldiers. These were men for the most part who could barely afford to buy the most basic weapons that the law required them to supply for all male members of the household. The many men who were so poor that they could not otherwise afford arms were provided guns at public expense, but only in exchange for performing public service. John Shy likened their obligation to labor to pay for their arms to the English working class which had to labor in the working-houses to compensate for charitable support.[26]

The principal military commanders ordinarily held the position of colonial governor, a title well established in England. His military deputies carried the title of councilors. In time of actual war in New England the governors frequently asked for and received the support of various town and city officials, men who often doubled as militia officers. Together, these men constituted the council of war.[27]

By 1641 both the home government and various local authorities in New England had come to the conclusion that a permanent and standing militia was indispensable for the protection of the inhabitants. A publication entitled *An Abstract of the Laws of New England as They are Now Established* concluded that for the best protection of the county, "First, a law [is] to be made for the training of all the men in the country fit to bear arms, unto the exercise of military discipline. . . ." The only other measure suggested for colonial defense was "and withal, another law to be made for the maintenance of military officers and forts." [28]

The New England Confederation, formed in 1643, was a primarily military organization consisting of New Plymouth, Massachusetts Bay, Connecticut, New Haven, Cornwall [Maine], and King's Province [a disputed area in southern New England]. This was essentially the same area as James II reorganized in 1686-89 as the Dominion of New England. It was devised as for "mutual safety and welfare," a self-defense program based on the colonial militias of these member provinces. Delegates met in Boston and adopted a written

---

26 Shy, *Toward Lexington,* 3.
27 Morton, Louis, "The Origins of American Military Policy," *Military Affairs,* 22 [1958]: 75-82; Daniel Boorstin. *Americans: The Colonial Experience*. Vintage, 1958, 341-72; Shy, *Toward Lexington,* 3-4.
28 *An Abstract of the Laws of New England as They are Now Established.* William Aspinwall, ed. London: Aspinwall, 1641, chapter 3.

constitution which formed The United Colonies of New England. Each colony retained its own system of managing internal affairs. Questions of war and peace were decided by eight commissioners representing Massachusetts, Plymouth, Connecticut and New Haven. Any six commissioners constituted a working majority. The commissioners met at least once a year and more frequently if there were problems brewing within its area of design.[29]

Expenses for the defensive system were borne by the colonies in proportion to the male population between ages sixteen and sixty, that is, of men of the proper age to serve in the militia. Massachusetts certainly bore the bulk of the expenses and had the vast majority of men subject to militia service, yet its commissioners carried no greater weight than the smaller colonies. The confederation would make, or at least approve, all appointments of officers and designate an overall commander-in-chief. Ordinarily, confederation troops were to be under the command of the ranking officer of the colony in which the troops were presently deployed.[30]

In 1653 the council met at Boston to consider "what number of soldiers might be requisite, if God called the Collonies to make warr against the Dutch." It named as captain commander John Leverett of Boston and apportioned its force of five hundred men as follows: Massachusetts Bay, 333; Plymouth, 60; Connecticut, 65; and New Haven, 42.

A major problem occurred for the confederation in 1653 when Massachusetts Bay refused to approve a war against the Dutch. Without its men and monetary contributions the union could not operate effectively. Initially, Massachusetts opposed the admission of Narragansett Bay [Rhode Island] and Cornwall [Maine] because the inhabitants held heterodox religious views. After 1664, when New Haven was annexed to Connecticut, the quotas and representation of the two confederation members was combined. At that point the constitution was amended to allow for meetings once ever three years instead of annually. The federation simultaneously went into a precipitous declined, but it revived briefly after a major threat from the native aborigine appeared. Between 1645 and 1650, and again in 1675, it waged

---

29 Adams, John Quincy, ed. *The New England Confederacy A Discourse delivered before the Massachusetts Historical Society, at Boston, on the 29th of May 1843; In Celebration of the Second Centennial of that Event.* Charles C. Little and James Brown, 1843.
30 *Plymouth Col. Rec.*, 1: 360.

war on the Narragansetts.[31] It operated most successfully during King Philip's War (1675-76), coordinating the defense of the region. In 1684 the charter of Massachusetts Bay was withdrawn and the confederation came to an end.

The Confederation had assumed the power to negotiate arms and gunpowder contracts, and to contract for maintenance and repair of the confederation's arms. Arms and supplies were to be stored in several convenient locations, with access to these materials of war granted to all members. It had sought the authority to declare war on Amerindian tribes on behalf of all members and to regulate the Indian trade and license Indian traders. It had sought the power to negotiate alliances with the various Amerindian tribes and to send negotiators to settle inter-tribal disputes. The confederation legally could take no action until at least six members approved, although this was not always the actual case.[32]

New England was more than sufficiently rich to sustain its militia. When it deployed men on the frontier it found that a town could feed, house, and otherwise provide for a considerable number of men. Most towns could contribute a company or two of militia to the general effort while retaining sufficient strength to defend themselves. Most towns had one or more fortified buildings that served as a base of operations when the militia was deployed in the area; and as places of refuge if the town came under Amerindian attack.

New England frequently offered its militiamen various incentives for performing their duties well. Although these colonies did not have large blocks of land to donate, but they did offer occasional bounties in land, notably in Maine. The colonies generally did not have to offer scalp bounties in order to mobilize militiamen, but again, on occasion, they did so. Too, there were possibilities of militiamen obtaining plunder; and others obtained money from the sales of Amerindian captives as slaves.

In 1688 the King James II was expelled, nominally because he kept a standing army in violation of Parliament's orders and for being sympathetic to Roman Catholics and to the French. Parliament passed a Mutiny Act, setting up courts-martial and imposing military law for periods of up to six months. There was no appeal to either

---

31 *Plymouth Col. Rec.,* 5: 74-76; 9: 12, 22, 45, 105; 10: 357-58; Mass. Col. Rec., 3: 39, 311; 5: 69.
32 *Plymouth Col. Rec.,* 9: 27.

the courts or Parliament and we may view this action as the beginning of true, sovereign parliamentary supremacy.

Parliamentary response provided, among other things, that the king could not keep a standing army in the time of peace. The basic assumption was that Parliament would control the militia while the monarch would command the standing army. Parliament would fund the military on an annual basis through the conventional budgetary process. In April 1689 the colonists of New England decided to endorse in the change of government by ousting royalist and reactionary Governor Edmund Andros (1637-1714).[33] The provincial authorities also ordered the arrest of royalist officers serving in Andros's army. Without their leaders, the army dissolved. A popular leader, Jacob Leisler, declared himself to be acting lieutenant-governor, to serve until the pleasure of Parliament become known. Dutch settlers in Albany (who were also under Andros's control) refused to recognize Leisler's dubious claim, choosing to rule themselves through a popularly elected town assembly. Only a militia remained to protect the borders, restrain and pacify the Amerindians and maintain order.[34]

The Dominion of New England "fulfilled the expectations of the Lords of Trade as a solution of the colonial problem of defense." It checked Indian encroachments and strengthened the alliance with the Iroquois. Andros's garrisoning of the frontier and his aggressive military ventures "made New England formidable to its enemies."[35] When the Dominion of New England collapsed, the new government in England delayed the formulation of imperial policy for the defense of the colonies. The Lords of Trade were insisting on reestablishing a consolidated government over the northern colonies, which they interpreted to include New England, New York, and New Jersey, under a single governor-general. However, this plan of reconsolidation was left unresolved because of the effective opposition led by the New England agents in London.[36]

The New England Puritans could claim victory only to the extent that they had succeeded in maintaining their status as a separate

---

33 Sosin, Jack. *English America and the Revolution of 1688: Royal Administration and the Structure of Provincial Government.* University of Nebraska Press, 1982, pp. 70-72.
34 Brodhead, James. *History of the State of New York.* Harper & Brothers, 1871, pp. 266-70.
35 Barnes, Viola. *Dominion of New England.* Kennikat, 1960, p. 229.
36 Ibid., p. 262.

colonies. Still, for a variety of good reasons, substantial opinion existed for re-establishing the Dominion. There was general agreement that any new dominion must shed its autocratic features. On 25 January 1691, a group of forty-five of the leading citizens of Massachusetts petitioned the King to appoint "a Governor and Council over us to administer the Government with an elected Assembly . . . and as many of the little provinces as seem good to you may be united under one Governor for mutual defence and security."[37]

In July 1691 New York Governor Henry Sloughter (died 1691), claiming that he had the backing of the council and General Assembly, expressed the same desire.[38] On 14 May 1692 William Phips (1651-1695) arrived at Boston carrying a parliamentary commission naming him as captain-general, governor and commander in chief of the militia for Rhode Island and Providence Plantations, Connecticut, the King's Province, Massachusetts and New Hampshire estates.[39] This was a plan the New England colonies opposed with great vigor because these provinces claimed that they alone controlled their own militias. They claimed there was no legal provision for subordinating the provincial militias to any exterior authority.[40]

Meanwhile, the colonists sought to create a military union on their own, prompted by the French and Indian hostilities along the New York and Maine frontiers in 1689. These incursions caught the northern colonies unprepared. To meet the emergency, attempts were made to reinstate a regional military union of much the same sort as the New England Confederation. Mutual military support was the theme of the times. In July 1689 Massachusetts Governor Bradstreet requested that Connecticut authorities to "be ready to yield all necessary assistance when desired according to the rules of our ancient union and confederation."[41] But the Confederation was not revitalized. Robert Livingston, writing from Hartford, speaking for many,

---

37 "Address of Divers Gentlemen, Merchants and Others of Boston, to the King," dated 25 January 1691, *Calendar of State Papers: America and West Indies*, 13: 212.
38 *Calendar of State Papers: America and West Indies,* 13: 514.
39 Lounsberry, Alice. *Sir William Phips*. Scribner's, 1941.
40 Gersham Bulkeley, "Will and Doom, or, the Miseries of Connecticut by and under an Usurped and Arbitrary Power" [1692] in *Collections of the Connecticut Historical Society,* (1861) 3: 240f.
41 "Order of Simon Bradstreet, Governor of the Massachusetts Convention," dated 17 July 1689, *Connecticut Archives*, 2: 10.

argued that "it will be very requisite that the united Colonies take Inspection of all affairs with us, since their interest and ours are so inseparable . . . "[42]

Connecticut and Rhode Island would not allow Phips to recruit volunteers, let alone draft men, from their militia on grounds that their charters granted them exclusive and inviolable rights to control and deploy their own militias. Phips appealed to the king, arguing that "you will not be soe unmindfull of your old neighbours." This failed to yield any results. The Rhode Island Assembly refused to recognize Phips as commander over the colony's militia and petitioned the crown for recognition of its charter rights. The Attorney General and Committee of Trade agreed to uphold Rhode Island's constitutional stand, but reaffirmed the Attorney General's opinion of 1690 that the crown retained the power to appoint a commander in chief over any part of a colony's militia. Thus, in time of invasion the king or his delegate could take charge of whatever forces required. Phips made no overt move to assume command over the militia of the colonies[43].

In May 1693, the crown ordered Benjamin Fletcher (1640-1703), governor of Pennsylvania, West Jersey, and New York, to take command of the Connecticut militia for an expedition against Canada. It told Phips to "consult and advise" with Fletcher. East Jersey and Pennsylvania refused to respond to Fletcher's demands for money and troops.[44] In October 1693 Fletcher, accompanied by two members of the New York Council, traveled to Hartford to establish his commission as commander of the Connecticut militia. Having learned of Fletcher's intentions earlier, the Connecticut General Court dispatched Fitz-John Winthrop to England to secure confirmation of the charter. The General Court took the position that Fletcher's commission could not supersede the powers that the Connecticut Charter granted to the colony over its own over the militia. "We are still willing to doe our proportion with our neighbours in such public charge wherein we are equally concerned," the Connecticut General Court informed Fletcher, but other colonies must do their share. Connecticut argued that it had already done more than its part by contributing to the garrisons at Albany and Deerfield.[45]

---

42 Dated 9 May 1690, in *New York Colonial Documents*, 3: 729.
43 *Massachusetts Archives*, 2: 211-12; Herbert L. Osgood, *The American Colonies in the Eighteenth Century*, 3 vols. Macmillan, 1904-07, 1: 100-03.
44 Osgood, American Colonies, 1: 102-03; *New York Colonial Documents*, 4: 13.
45 *The Acts and Resolves of the Province of Massachusetts Bay*. 17 vols. State of

Fletcher, in a letter to the Lords of Trade, warned that Connecticut's obstinacy would lead to a French victory in North America. "These People of Connecticut are in a greate fright the noise of a Quo Warranto or A sharp Letter from theire Majesties will reduce Them the wisest and Richest of them Desire to bee under the Kings imediate Government."[46] Fletcher called a general conference of the governors to obtain pledges of troops and financial aid from each colony. The Board of Trade authorized to Fletcher to issue a call for troops from New York, Rhode Island, Massachusetts, Pennsylvania, Maryland, and Virginia. Moreover, the crown authorized the appointment of a chief commander to order the combined provincial militias in time of war. The crown also ordered the colonies to contribute troops or other assistance upon request of the governor of New York.

Several of the colonies were outraged at this assertion of English power over the colonial militias. The Rhode Island Assembly resolved that "in time of peace, and when the danger is over, the militia within each of the said provinces ought, as we humbly conceive, to be under the government and disposition of the respective Governors of the Colonies, according to their Charters."[47] Another negative provincial reaction was financial. For example, the Maryland House of Delegates only reluctantly voted a small appropriation and elusively talked of the possibility of future free will donations.[48] The London Board of Trade considered the establishment of a colonial military union to be of paramount importance.

On 30 September 1696 the Board considered various proposals along that line from the colonies. John Nelson, Governor Fletcher of New York and Governor Nicholson of Maryland offered plans that, while intriguing, were also insufficient or unacceptable. The Board concluded that in wartime all provincial militia should be placed under one a single authority who would bear the title of captain general, who would be invested with the powers of a royal governor.

American colonial representatives then appeared before the Board of Trade, but they were unable to agree on a united front that they would present before the board. Edmund Harrison, Henry Ashurst, William Phips, representing New England and Daniel Coxe

---

Massachusetts, 1869-1910, 7: 418.
46 Governor Fletcher to John Trenchard, dated 10 November 1693, quoted in John G. Palfrey. *History of New England.* 4 vols. Boston, 1890, 4: 225-27.
47 *Rhode Island Colonial Records*, 3: 296.
48 Andrews, Mathew P. *History of Maryland.* Chicago: Clarke, 1925, 209-10.

of New York argued for the creation of a governor general with civil as well as well as military jurisdiction. Fitz-John Winthrop reiterated Connecticut's position based upon the charter rights it held that precluded tampering with its militia. Chidley Brooke and William Nicoll of New York favored a stronger union than any yet proposed. The Board of Trade feared the consequences of voiding the charters of Rhode Island and Connecticut without due legal process. Thus, the Board decided to recommend a military union superimposed by the Crown. In February 1697 an order by the king-in-council directed the establishment of a military union of the four New England colonies, New York, and West New Jersey under a captain-general.[49]

The first appointment of captain-general went to Richard Coote, first Earl of Bellomont (1636-1701) in the Irish peerage. Bellomont had powerful support, for among those backing him were William III, Lord Shrewsbury and Sir Henry Ashurst. It was a good appointment for Bellomont was acceptable to the New England and New York. While his political title was Governor of New York, Massachusetts and New Hampshire, in reality, Bellomont received command over all the militia of the northern colonies. That command could be exercised only during wartime. Bellomont did not reach New York until April 1698 and did not take over the reins of the Massachusetts government until May 1699. Unfortunately, his first great commitment was not military but criminal. He arrived just in time to become embroiled in the Captain Kidd affair.[50] He had no success in gaining recognition of his military powers in Rhode Island. Whatever chance he may have had to succeed there initially was soon lost as he became obsessed with enforcement of the highly unpopular Navigation Acts.[51] More destructive yet, he became entangled in the complex politics, largely of New York, that had also undone his predecessor, Benjamin Fletcher. Bellomont died suddenly in March 1701, and with him died also the plan for military unity.[52]

---

49 Osgood, *American Colonies*, 1: 151-52, 267-69; *New York Colonial Documents*, 4: 259-61; *Calendar of State Papers: America and West Indies*, 15: 318.
50 Hanna, Archibald, Jr. "New England Military Institutions, 1693-1750" Ph. D. dissertation, Yale University, 1951; Frederic de Peyster. *The Life and Administration of Richard, Earl of Bellomont*. 2 vols. New York Historical Society, 1879, 1: 31-32, 57.
51 See de Peyster, *Earl of Bellomont*.
52 Palfrey, John Gorham. *History of New England*. Little, Brown, 1875, 4: 171-77, 216.

Renewed call for a central military authority for New England came as the colonies prepared to enter Queen Anne's War. Joseph Dudley (1647-1720) had received his commission in 1702 as Governor of Massachusetts and New Hampshire. With this was his appointment as captain general with authority over all the New England militia in time of war. He was also vice-admiral of Rhode Island.[53] Dudley found it impossible to weld together an inter-colonial military system. New England had two objections to his appointment. First, there had objections to his previous service as the first governor of the Dominion of New England. He was also closely tied to the established high church party in England. Rhode Island and Connecticut refused to send troops beyond the frontier of the Connecticut Valley during the early phase of Queen Anne's War. Connecticut disbanded its militia in 1704 without Dudley's authorization. When told to obey the orders of the Massachusetts Governor, Connecticut refused. In late 1706 and early 1707 Dudley appealed to Fitz-John Winthrop, begging him to use his powers of persuasion to enlist the support of Connecticut in the combined provincial expedition being assembled to capture Port Royal in Acadia. Winthrop replied that the Connecticut Assembly would not cooperate because there was nothing about that expedition that would benefit the colony. Rhode Island also denied Dudley's military authority over its militia.[54]

Professor John Shy, a leading critic of the American colonial militia system, observed that, about 1710, "it would be wrong to idealize the New England militia, but it would be equally mistaken not to recognize that there the institution had retained its vitality."[55] Toward the end of Queen Anne's War (1702-1713) Governor Joseph Dudley could boast that his militia system had achieved two goals. First, it successfully defended its own frontiers and most settlements from French and Amerindian attack. Second, it had supplied significant troop strength to assist the English expeditions against French Canada.[56]

---

53 Kimball, Everett. *The Public Life of Joseph Dudley.* New York: Harvard Historical Studies, 1911, pp. 15: 75, 120, 143-48.
54 Kimball, *Joseph Dudley,* pp. 143-47; Palfrey, *New England,* 4: 359-62; Harry M. Ward. *Unite or Die: Intercolony Relations, 1690-1763.* Port Washington: Kennikat, 1971, ch. 2.
55 Shy, *Toward Lexington,* p. 14.
56 Kimball. *Joseph Dudley,* pp. 124-25, 183.

The Political Pulpit

Military exercise was closely associated with the Sabbath, with drills often following church services. The Puritan clergy had no problem with being closely connected to the military since Calvinism accepted the Old Testament view of God as the warring Jehovah ready to smite his enemies and protect those with whom he had a covenant. Many a sermon given on militia day began with the words of second Chronicles, to be "ready prepared for war."[45] Exercise with arms was a godly thing for a man to do as well as being a way to train one's self physically.

John Calvin (1509-1564), founder of Puritanism, had taught that war is the way of life in the material world, with God's people pitted against the devil and his minions. God's people must be ever militant and constantly armed in a physical, as well as material, sense. Christian warfare is certainly not confined to the spiritual realms, but finds real struggles in worldly combat. Some Christians will experience only spiritual tests while others will be called to the front in war. Calvin obscures any differences to be found between physical and spiritual warfare. The Christian in every sense is called upon to gird his loins, take hold of his shield, and don his armor. Every Christian is a soldier and has a role in the army of Christ.

Paul of Tarsus warned us that our struggle is not with flesh and blood, but with the princes of the air, with the powers of darkness, and spiritual wickedness, forthwith bids us put on that armor capable of sustaining so great and dangerous a contest. We have been forewarned that an enemy relentlessly threatens us, an enemy who is the very embodiment of rash boldness, of military prowess, of crafty wiles, of untiring zeal and haste, of every conceivable weapon and of skill in the science of warfare.[57]

It is difficult for most of us to imagine that we are completely in the right, that our cause is unquestionably just, and our leaders are heaven-led, nut so it was for the Puritans. Relying heavily upon the Hebrew Bible, as did all Calvinism, they read "When you go out to war against your enemies and you see horses and chariots and an army greater than your own, you shall not be afraid of them, for the Lord, your God, who brought you up from the land of Egypt, will be

---

57 Ephesians 6: 12-13; John Calvin. *Institutes of the Christian Religion*. John T. McNeil, ed. Westminster Press, 1967, 1: 73.

with you. When you are drawing near to battle, the priest shall come forward and speak to the army, and say to them, "Hear, O Israel! Today you are drawing near for battle against your enemies. Do not be weak-hearted or afraid, alarmed or frightened by them."[58] Following God's prescription in the Book of Deuteronomy, they were to kill not only those male enemies who resisted, but also all members of certain tribes. They were also commanded to take spoils from the enemy and enjoy those goods.[59]

The New England Puritans built churches, towns, along with an entire commonwealth on a contractual model. Here, individuals voluntarily promised to accept Biblical law in exchange for benefits that would naturally flow from acceptance of God's will. Free will acceptance was the quintessential ingredient in this contract. The Puritans believed that meaningful obedience could only grow out of voluntary consent, never out of coercion. The Reverend Thomas Hooker insisted that the man who desired to enter a social covenant had "willingly [to] binde and ingage himselfe to each member of that society. . . or else a member actually he is not." Likewise, the trainbands were a covenanted organization based on voluntarism. The Puritans had no cause to fear that their militia would abuse its power by oppressing the towns or by collect [60]

As Puritanism expanded in England and gained adherents so Calvin's call to arms found support in religious writings. The eminent preacher John Downame (1571-1652) produced an important and influential tract, *The Christian Warfare*, in 1609, in which he warned that Christians must not grow too fond of the material world for it is the arena of combat between the devil and God. He urged each man to become a soldier of Christ in both the physical and physical senses. Each reborn Christian will be awakened to the knowledge that he must stand firm physically and spiritually in face of God's enemies. It was Downame who popularized the image of Nehemiah's workers who worked on the temple while girding his loins against the enemy. All Christians must emulate Nehemiah by being both worker and militiaman. He urged all the faithful to heed the words of Paul in Ephesians: "Put on the whole armor of God that ye be able to stand

---

58 Deuteronomy 20: 1-3.
59 Deuteronomy 20: 10-18.
60 Hooker, Thomas. *A Survey of the Summe of Church Discipline*. London, 1648, I: 47.

against the assaults of the devil."[61]

One recent scholar concluded that "the combined emphasis upon aggressive Christian combat, which received the imprimatur of Bible and minister . . . shaped the expectations of New England's earliest settlers in the seventeenth century." The ministers adopted an aggressive style, used strong rhetoric, depicted heroic biblical figures fighting God's wars, and painted glorious pictures of the triumph of good over evil. Discussion of great biblical war heroes was designed, of course, to inspire parallel lives among the militiamen of New England.[62]

As William Haller observed, the Puritan imagination saw the spiritual life as pilgrimage and battle, and "the main business of Christian wayfaring was war." To the Puritans, the elect soul was a "Soldier of Christ." The spiritual attitude which the preachers endeavored to inculcate was one of active struggle on the part of the individual against his own weakness. The supreme image, for that purpose, they sought to impress upon the minds of the people was that of the soldier enlisted under the banners of Christ . . . they made the atonement signify the appointment of the elect soul to join with Christ in the war against the eternal enemy."[63]

What would the Lord God permit his people do if their enemies burned their crops, slaughtered their cattle, abducted their wives and children, and killed and tortured the inhabitants of the land He had given them? One early work answered the question by calling the people to arms. Captain Edward Johnson (1599-1672) was a joiner by vocation, preacher by avocation, and militiaman by necessity. He became an expert in the use of artillery and was founder of the new settlement of Woburn. He wrote his masterpiece *The Wonder-Working Providence of Sion's Saviour* in New England about 1653, partially to persuade others to join his settlement and largely to extol the

---

61 Ephesians, 6: 11. Downame, John. *The Christian Warfare: Written Especially for Their Sakes who are Exercised in the Spirituall Conflict of Tentations, and are Afflicted in Conscience in the Sight Ande Sense of Their Sinnes* (1609). See also John Downame. *The Christian Warfare Against the Deuill, World and Flesh...* W. Stansby, 2013.

62 Agearn, Marie L. *The Rhetoric of War: Training Day, the Militia and the Military Sermon.* Greenwood, 1989, 23.

63 Haller, William. *Rise of Puritanism; Or, the Way to the New Jerusalem as Set Forth in Pulpit and Press From Thomas Cartwright to John Lilburne and John Milton.* Harper & Row, 1957, pp. 142, 150-51.

greatness of God who had delivered His people out of bondage and into the new promised land.[64] Johnson saw the migration in military terms, calling the settlers soldiers employed in God's service. To Johnson's way of thinking, God in holy scripture had provided all the military knowledge that His people needed to defeat the devil's forces. The Bible was the only book on military tactics and strategy humans needed. Johnson's book used military terminology and vocabulary familiar to the men of his time. He dwelled, with some obvious delight and pleasure, on the bloodier parts of the Old Testament, showing that God intended that war be unrelenting and filled with slaughter of Satan's followers.[65]

Johnson noted the parallels between the holy commonwealth of New England and spiritual biography. According to Johnson, individual salvation and an earthly millennium are contingent upon one another: "Assuredly the spiritual fight is chiefly to be attended, and the other [the literal] not neglected, having a neer dependancy one upon the other, especially at this time."[66]

Johnson's biblical and practical arguments, closely followed Calvin and Downame. These arguments influenced nearly all ministers and writers for the next hundred years. Later writers followed both Johnson's form and substance. He effectively combined Biblical rhetoric with law of the colonies, giving justification to the natural inclination that men have to kill their enemies. Other works with similar themes and arguments followed.

Johnson and his followers were concerned about the demonic forces which oppressed them in that wilderness, which evil spirits they identified with their theological enemies. They saw the world as a real battleground with the forces of good pitted against the forces of evil. They denounced his enemies in his *Wonder Working Providence* in the strongest possible terms, suggesting their probable association with the devil. The Puritans were God's militia engaged in holy warfare against Jehovah's eternal enemies. Johnson himself claimed that the enemies of Massachusetts were "malignant adversaries," that is, infested by Satan. Moreover, his opponents were members of the

---

64 Johnson, Edward. *The Wonder Working Providence of Sion's Saviour in New England.* London: Kyngston, 1654.
65 Gallagher, Edward J., "The" Wonder-Working Providence" as Spiritual Biography.," *Early American Literature,* 10.1 (1975), pp. 75-87.
66 Johnson, Edward. *Wonder Working Providence,* Essex Institute Historical Collections, 1968 p. 230.

"malignant and anti-christian party," full of the "spirit of malignity," and anxious to vent their "wicked malignity" upon a poor, wandering people. The Devil had stirred up his minions "to take upon them this long Voyage," and eventually to ravage the Massachusetts colony.[67]

A generation later, during King Philip's War, preachers suggested that the saints take refuge behind "protective shields of spiritual walls." Some, perhaps more practical, interpreted this as meaning that the towns ought to build stockades. Some of the elders suggested building a wall eight feet high stretching from the Charles to the Concord River.[68]

The more worldly clergy agreed with the politicians about the efficacy of a physical wall, suggesting in their sermons that the correct model was found in the Book of Nehemiah. This leader labored mightily in constructing the walls of the temple, building them as strong as materials and technology permitted. While engaged in this labor, Nehemiah and his men remained armed, ready to unsheath the sword in their own defense. Just as the Christian put on his spiritual armor, so he also was to arm himself physically.[69] Proper physical facilities combined with a well-trained citizen army would create all the protection God's people would need to survive.

There were certain practical aspects of combining military training with Sunday services. Preachers could subject their flock to prolonged sermons that often took several hours to deliver. Puritans endured these homilies because they were the center of the religious service and because they represented an exercise in literacy and literature. Politics and religion entered into militia service and organization. During the religious quarrel over the Anne Hutchinson heresy, some men refused to march with their units as long as Pastor John Wilson served as a chaplain, while others indicated their unwillingness to serve if Wilson were dismissed. New England's ministers argued that the Christian defense of true religion was vitally interconnected with the defense of the colonies. Both matters could be advanced by combining arms with a Calvinist interpretation of biblical text. Many chose to back their words with action by marching as chaplains with the troops during war or punitive expeditions against the Amerindians.

---

67 Johnson, *Wonder Working Providence*, pp. 122, 124, 132, 147, 148, 152.
68 *Mass. Archives,* 68: 174-80.
69 Ephesians 6: 11-17.

On 3 June 1678, Boston minister Samuel Nowell (1634-1688) delivered a discourse to his congregation based on the image of biblical patriarch Abraham as the first great man of arms fighting in the Lord's cause. He promised that abundant blessings would flow upon such men as served faithfully in the militia. Typical of the second generation political pulpit, following Johnson, was Nowell's "Abraham in Arms" in which he described the importance of the armed citizenry.

> God's vineyards hath no other walls, but only our Souldiery, that and our Poverty. We have no walled towns, as they have in other places, our Forts and Castles are contemptible. We have not any bank of money to hire Souldiers; our strength by sea is small & for friendship and favour in the world with any that should help us, is not much, or our friends lye too far off to help us in time of need.[70]

Nowell continued, suggesting that, with God's help, there was no obstacle that could overcome the arms of the Puritans. God's people were clad in spiritual armor that no arrow could penetrate or spear violate.

Cotton Mather (1663-1728) was one of the best known political-religious philosophers of Puritanism and arguably the finest and most influential American theologian of the period. On 1 September 1689 he delivered a long and powerful sermon urging his fellow Puritan to smite their Amerindian adversaries, justifying the punitive expedition on biblical grounds. Like his Calvinist predecessors, Mather thought it was the duty of all believers, but especially the elect, to defend their own territory. Incursions into their land was caused by Satan, in his disguise as the French king, and his devils under the guise of papist soldiers. These legions of the prince of darkness had seduced the innocent savages into playing their evil game. Protestants must rise and do battle with such evil figures. Mather followed St. Augustine on his doctrine of the just war, seeing the wars against the French and their Amerindian allies as the children of light pitted against the children of darkness. Mather referred to the Amerindians variously as Canaanites, Medianites, and "barbarous heathen." Those

---

[70] Nowell, Samuel, "Abraham in Arms, or, the First Religious General with his Army Engaging in a War for which He Has Wisely Prepared and by Which Not Only an Eminent Victory Was Obtained, but a Blessing Gained Also." Boston: Foster, 1678. The best source for early documents and sermons is the Early American Imprints, two series. Hereinafter, E. A. I., 1st series, no. 256.

killed or maimed in such a campaign might expect a stern but just God to reward them for their sacrifices on His behalf.[71]

During King William's War (1689-1697), Reverend Benjamin Wadsworth (1670-1737) offered a blessing to the militiamen who were marching toward French positions in the North, entitled "A Letter of Wholesome Counsels Directed to Christian Souldiers Going Forth to War," exhorting them to behave as warriors of biblical times. The war generally inspired ministers to focus upon worldly strife and the temporal duties of the militiaman to an extent not seen in more than a generation. This emphasis was to be repeated in later wars with France, so much so that one might think that each new generation of pastors had dusted off and delivered again the famous sermons of this generation.[72]

King George's War (1740-1748) again brought forth support for the militia from the New England political pulpit. On 1 August 1745, Nathaneal Walter (1711-1776) delivered a powerful sermon at the Old Boston Church, "The Character of a True Patriot," in which he dwelled on the subject of the Christian's dual duty of serving God and his king by entering into combat with the devil and his earthly legions.[73] Thomas Prince (1687-1758) followed on 27 November 1746 with a condemnation of cowards and a promise of sainthood to true patriot militiamen, delivered at the South Church in Boston.[74] On 17 June 1745, Jared Eliot (1685-1763), pastor at Killingworth, repeated the same basic themes to the militiamen of his congregation.[75]

In 1732 Oliver Peabody introduced the heroic image of David the warrior king into the literature of the New England pulpit. Begin-

---

71 Cotton Mather penned several influential works on the Indian wars. *The History of a Long War with Indian Savages and their Directors and Abettors*. Boston: Green, 1714. E. A. I. 1st series, no. 1688; *The Present State of New England, Considered in a Discourse on the Necessities and Advantages of a Public Spirit in Every Man*. Boston: Green, 1690. Photostat Americana, 1st series, 1936; *Souldiers Counselled and Comforted, a Discourse Delivered unto Some Parts of the Forces Engaged in the Just War of New England against the Northern and Eastern Indians* [1689]. Louisville, Ky: Lost Cause Press, 1967.

72 Wadsworth, Benjamin. *A Letter of Wholesome Counsels Directed to Christian Souldiers Going Forth to War*. Boston: Green, 1709. E. A. I., 1st series, no. 1438.

73 Walther, Nathaneal. *The Character of a True Patriot*. Boston: D. Heachman, 1745, E. A. I., 1st series, no. 5706.

74 Price, Thomas. *Salvation of God*. Early American Imprint, 1st series, no. 5856.

75 Eliot, Jared. *God's Marvellous Kindness*. New London, Ct.: Green, 1745.

ning with 2 Samuel 1:18, Peabody developed the image of the godly youth who slew Goliath and taught his people the use of arms. David trained his men in news ways of waging war, which lessons were still valuable to the militia of New England. Peabody described the ideally trained militiaman.

> [H]e will be a finished soldier, that can find, fight and conquer his enemies in the thicket of the Woods; and immediately fall into a marshalled and regular Army, or into a disciplined troop, and fight and overcome in an open Field; and also excel again on the Mighty Deep, and understand the best Manner of fighting on the sea.[76]

In 1741 William Hooper (1674-1767), a late Puritan clergyman, delivered a sermon entitled "Christ the Life of True Believers and their Appearance in Glory" in which he argued that men who failed to defend their native land had little chance of gaining salvation. True Christians were required to take up arms against the heathen (Amerindians) and heretics (Roman Catholic French).[77]

After news of clashes with the French and their occupation of the Ohio Territory was received, all the northern colonies called for a day of fasting and prayer that the land might be delivered from the French and their Amerindian allies. In Newark, New Jersey, on 1 January 1755, Reverend Aaron Burr (1716-1767) delivered a long sermon calling upon "the Lord Jehovah . . . to smite his enemies as in the days of old." Burr thought that, should the Protestants unite in their effort and make appropriate offerings and prayerful petitions to God, they would surely be rewarded with victory.[78]

New England's clergy was not going to be outdone by a mainstream Protestants from New Jersey. Reverend Samuel Checkley (1723-1768) preached a major and lengthy sermon, "The Duty of God's People When Engaged in War," in Boston soon after to the local militia. So popular was that discourse among the local politicians that he was invited to deliver it to militia units throughout the province of Massachusetts.[79] William Currie (1709-1803) preached a similar ser-

---

76 Peabody, Oliver. *Essay to Revive and Encourage Military Exercises*. Boston: Eddes & Gill, 1732.
77 Hooper, William, *Christ the Life of True Believers and their Appearance in Glory.* Boston: Fowle, 1741.
78 Burr, Aaron. *A Discourse Delivered at Newark in New Jersey on 1 January 1755, Being the Day Set Aside for Solemn Fasting and Prayer.* New York: Gaine, 1755. News Micro 961.
79 Checkley, Samuel. *The Duty of God's People When Engaged in War*. Boston:

mon at Radnor Church on 7 January 1747.[80] Reverend Peter Clark (1694-1768) prepared a sermon with a theme similar to Checkley's. Entitled "Religion to be Minded Under the Greatest Perils of Life," this discourse also exhorted Christians to do their duty, including faithful service in the militia.[81]

Clark's and Checkley's sermons were buttressed by a powerful sermon delivered by Reverend Sylvanus Conant (1720-1777) in his "The Art of War, the Gift of God." It asserted that in the Old Testament, God had drawn a blueprint for victory in wars in which His people defended divine justice. God had instructed the Hebrew people in the art of war and inspired their leaders to use even the most unorthodox tactics to win against their enemies. The art of war, it seems, was born in the mind of the Heavenly Father, to be used to advance His causes.[82] An anonymously written and printed largely religious discourse on much the same themes appeared about this same time under the title, "New England's Misery, the Procuring Cause and a Strong Remedy."[83]

Reverend Samuel Cooper (1725-1783) delivered another powerful and politically charged sermon before the governor of Massachusetts in the summer of 1759. Militia service, he argued, was the duty of every Christian male. He thought that the most severe legal penalties and social ostracism could be directed against those who shirked their duty. Cooper assured the governor that he was properly discharging the functions of his office when he sent the militia into battle against God's enemies and the unconverted heathen.[84]

Samuel Chandler's (1723-1768) Thanksgiving Day sermon, given on 29 November 1759, reminded the faithful that they must rejoice in the defeat of the papist French and be prepared at all times to repel false religion because God required that "true religion" be defended, if necessary by force of arms. Good Christians could be god-

---

Fowle, 1755. News Micro 961.
80 Currie, William. *A Sermon Preached in Radnor Church on Thursday, 7 January 1747*.... Philadelphia: Franklin & Head, 1748, E. A. I., 1st series, no. 6119.
81 Clark, Peter. *Religion to Be Minded Under the Greatest Perils of Life*. Boston: Kneeland, 1755. News Micro 961.
82 Conant, Sylvanus. *The Art of War, the Gift of God*. Boston: Edes & Gill, 1759. News Micro 961.
83 *New England's Misery, the Procuring Cause and a Strong Remedy Proposed*. Boston: Fowle & Draper, 1758.
84 Cooper, Samuel. *A Sermon Preached before His Excellency, Thomas Pownell*. Boston: Green & Russell, 1759. News Micro 961.

ly soldiers in righteous causes.[85]

The French surrender at Montreal occasioned an extensive response from the New England pulpit. The Seven Years' War being now terminated, we should expect to hear the kind of sermon preached by Reverend Amos Adams (1728-1775), at Roxbury, Massachusetts, on 25 October, and Nathaniel Appleton a few days later. While the principal theme of these sermons was thanksgiving for the safe return of many militiamen, victory over their ancient enemy, and the end of a long and costly war, the preachers universally used the occasion to exhort the citizen-soldiers to be prepared to continue to serve whenever danger threatened the country.[86]

On 6 March 1763, Pastor John Brown (1715-1766) preached a sermon on religious liberty and political freedom in which he urged all Christians to take up arms against the marauding Amerindians. In doing so, they were doing God's work and defending His people. Likewise, Protestants must rejoice in the defeat of the Catholic French and be ever vigilant lest they return to North America to threaten Protestantism.[87] Brown's position reminds one of John Milton's *Aeropagetica* in which he defended freedom of speech excpt for Catholics because they are loyal only to the pope.

When Anglican minister Anthony Benezet (1713-1784) delivered in Philadelphia a sermon entitled "Thoughts on the Nature of War and Its Repugnancy to Christian Life," the congregation virtually rebelled. Nothing could be farther from the Puritan theology tyhan pacifism. Throughout the land various newspapers summarized the sermon and it was printed by one of the larger and more prominent publishers of the day. Reaction to the sermon, especially in New England was strongly negative, appearing in various sermons, especially those delivered before militia companies, such as the Ancient Artillery Company of Boston.[88]

---

85   Chandler, Samuel. *A Sermon Preached at Gloucester, Thursday, 29 November 1759, Being the Day of Provincial Anniversary Thanksgiving.* Boston: Green & Russell, 1759. News Micro 961.

86   Adams, Amos. *Songs of Victory Detested by Human Compassion and Qualified with Christian Benevolence.* Boston: Edes & Gill, 1759. News Micro 961; Nathaniel Appleton. *A Sermon Preached on October 9, being a Day of Public Thanksgiving Occasioned by the Surrender of Montreal. . . .* Boston: Draper, 1760. E. A. I., 1st series, no. 8536.

87   Brown, John. *On Religious Liberty, a Sermon. . . .* Philadelphia: Davis & Reymers, 1763. E.A.I. 1st series, no. 9356.

88   Benezet, Anthony. Thoughts on the Nature of War and its Repugnancy to

We may summarize the themes of the political pulpit as follows. First, war spiritualizes the soldier by making him ponder his own mortality and his relationship to his Creator whom he might soon meet. Second, it brought each man into contact with the heroic figures of the Old Testament who then offered him a choice of role models for his own life, just as others may have been inspired by stories of the saints. The clergy stopped just short of condemning those who were cowardly in battle, but most agreed with Increase Mather that courage was a manifestation of God's grace, given to the elect. Many sermons emphasized the importance of behaving bravely in performance of all duties, especially militia duty. Third, it produced an archetype in ancient Israel and presented the parallel so clearly that all could see that New England constituted the New Jerusalem and the saints inhabiting the land were the new Chosen People.

Fourth, it reminded all that the Second Coming of Christ and what are generally known as millennial events were hard by the door, close at hand. Man should never stray from this vision when there would be the final clash between God and Satan, the Battle of Armageddon. Even that battle had its archetypes in the victories of Barak over the Canaanites and of Gideon over the Midianites. The battles in this new world just might be some of the tribulations noted in the apocalyptic view of St. John the Divine as immediately preceding this final battle. Fifth, ministers reminded the officers that the Bible offered the best and most reliable guide to many things, not the least important of which are military tactics and strategy. The men should take great comfort when their elected officers opted to follow the great leaders of the Hebrew Bible. There were, according to the ministers, great parallels between the way the native aborigine fought and the way enemies of Israel had waged war. Men should choose their officers for their virtue, godliness and intimate knowledge of scripture.

Sixth, it was the duty of every man to learn his trade and to practice it with patience and skill, but to also be a soldier in the Army of the Lord. We may recall the early emphasis, especially in Johnson, on Nehemiah and his men working on the temple while standing guard over their nation. In short, it was godly to be expert in war, ev-

---

Christian Life. Philadelphia: Millar, 1766. E. A. I., 1st series, 10,505. Among strong reactions were those published in the *Pennsylvania Ledger*, 10 October 1766, and the *Boston Gazette*, 22 October 1766.

ery Israelite in God's service is a man of war.[89]

Seventh, the clergy revived the notion that had plagued St. Augustine, St. Thomas Aquinas, and most of the commentators in the new field of international law, namely, what is the just war? It was clear that these men would not entertain the possibility that no war is just as was the premise of the pacifist sects, such as the Society of Friends. Pacifist Quakers became an object of frequent parody and ridicule, with at least two having been burned at the stake for proselytizing their beliefs in Massachusetts. Any war against God's enemies, notably the devil and his legions, would clearly be just. Likewise, wars against false religion, notably papism, were justified. The clergy appointed itself judge over such determination and classification. Friends and other pacifists had determined that very few, if any, of New England's wars could be found to have been unjustified.

Eighth, wars must also be fought justly, although there are notable biblical examples of Israel slaughtering all the enemy.[90] It is much better to be magnanimous in victory and charitable in peace. Neither should one fight an offensive war, although the clergy universally classified wars of retaliation and punishment as justified. A defensive war is lawful beyond dispute. Reverend Increase Mather (1639-1723), president of Harvard, commented on the just war.

> And in some cases men may be called to ingage in an Offensive War. This may be Lawful when their Liberties, Properties and Possessions are invaded. . . . Only it is to be remembered that an Offensive War is not to be undertaken but with the Consent and Authority of the Magistrates. The reason is because war is an act of Vindictive Justice and therefore must have the Countenance of those who are by their Office Revengers to Execute wrath on them that do Evil.[91]

Not all commentators agreed with Mather that the magistrates alone should decide when a war was justified. Some wished to engage the clergy since the question was a moral one. Others wished that the process would be more democratic, involving the whole community. The latter view was derived from William of Ockham, a fa-

---

89 2 Timothy 2:3
90 Survivors in war were frequently slaughtered as in: Judges 9:45; 2 Sam. 12: 31; and 2 Chron. 25:12. Others were carried into captivity, Num. 31:26. Some were even mutilated, Judges, 1:6.
91 Mather, Increase. *A Discourse Concerning the Grace of Courage*. Boston: Eddes, 1710

vorite of Martin Luther, who had argued that all moral and theological decisions should be made by the whole body of the faithful.

In the Puritan view, three men in addition to Nehemiah stand as archetypes of the military heroism required of New England militiamen. Abraham was the first great religious general and an archetype of Jesus Christ. Joshua completed the mission initially assigned to Moses, expelling the Canaanites from the Promised Land. David was the favored of God, prophet, poet and priest, but it was David the youthful military genius and conqueror of Goliath upon which the Puritan clergy dwelled. The preachers reminded the people how David instructed his flock in the use of arms and urged them to learn the use of the bow.[92]

Woven upon biblical imperatives, the minister's words commanded a central position in the militia rituals. During his service as a militiaman in 1686, bookseller John Dunton (1659-1733) recalled the prayer meetings. They began with a "solemn prayer in the field upon the day of training, [which] I never knew but in New England, where it seems to be a common custom. About three o'clock, both our exercise and prayers being over, we had a very noble dinner to which all the clergy were invited."[93]

Later militiamen recalled hearing and being inspired by such sermons. Sergeant David Holden (1738-1803) recalled serving in the Massachusetts militia and hearing sermons on the righteous cause and just war being fought against the French and their Amerindian allies.[94] As a young man, much afraid of death or permanent injury, Uriah How (1738-1758) kept a journal in which he recorded his innermost thoughts. How thought that the many sermons he heard while on service relieved him of much apprehension. Presumably, when he was killed in his twentieth year, he had been better prepared to meet his Maker because of the messages he had heard.[95] David B. Perry, born in 1741, was a teenager in the Seven Years War and much afraid of what might be his fate in battle. He, too, felt comforted by the mes-

---

92 2 Sam. 1: 17-27.
93 Dunton, John, "Dunton's Journal," in *Collections of the Massachusetts Historical Society,* 2d series, 2 [1814], p. 107.
94 Holden, David. *Journal Kept by Sergeant David Holden of Groton, Massachusetts, during the Latter Part of the French and Indian War.* Cambridge, Ma,: Wilson & Son, 1889.
95 How, Uriah. *A Discourse Written by Uriah How of Canaan in the Twentieth Year of His Age.* New Haven: Parker, 1761. E. A. I., 1st series, no. 41,202.

sage of the preachers who accompanied the militia. When he entered the patriot cause in the American Revolution, Perry urged his fellow soldiers to attend religious services, relating his own experience with the clergy in the earlier war.[96] Two other privates in the Massachusetts militia, men who served in both the Seven Years War and the Revolution, felt themselves to have been much inspired by the call to action issued by New England clergymen before and during enlistment.[97]

General Seth Pomeroy (1706-1777) and General Rufus Putnam (1738-1824) thought that their men in both the Seven Years War and the War for Independence had achieved far greater peace of mind than most other militiamen and soldiers because of the comfort offered by militantly military clergy who accompanied their troops.[98]

Funerals of prominent militia officers and of enlisted men killed in battle offered occasions to combine military parades with martial sermons. The dead man's comrades turned out in large numbers to parade and accompany the deceased to the grave. The precedent of firing volleys of musket shots over the grave seems to have been common practice by 1630. The clergy utilized the opportunity of such a funeral to laud the Christian soldier who serves God by smiting His enemies. Clergy frequently compared the wearing of physical armor in military service to the assumption of the armor of God in baptism. During the funeral service the deceased put away his metal armor and weapons to assume the spiritual armor of grace that God bestowed on His elect.

Massachusetts, along with the other colonies in New England set aside one or more days for training and disciplining the citizen-soldiers. This custom had been inherited from medieval England where similar days had been set aside for like purpose in each shire. When training day laws went unenforced the militias lapsed into mobs that were unable to coordinate their activities on the field of bat-

---

96 Perry, David B. *Recollections of an Old Soldier.* Tarrytown, NY: W. Abbatt, 1928; *Magazine of History*, extra no. 37: 1.
97 *Military Journals of Two Private Soldiers, 1758-1775.* Poughkeepsie, NY: Tomlinson, 1855.
98 Pomeroy, Seth. *Journal and Papers of Seth Pomeroy, Sometime General in the Colonial Service.* New York: Society of Colonial Wars in the State of New York, 1926, publication number 38; Rufus Putnam. *Journal of General Rufus Putnam Kept in Northern New York during Four Campaigns of the Old French and Indian War, 1757-1760.* Albany: Munsell, 1886.

tle and were unwilling to obey their officers. Occasionally, part of the training days was set aside to repair and build fortifications. A chaplain opened and closed the day with a prayer and occasionally with a sermon. The minister also enforced morality laws to such a degree that public drunkenness was all but unknown and the camp followers that commonly accompanied men in arms were also nowhere to be found.

During the French and Indian War a New York correspondent of the London-based *Public Advertiser* praised the moral character of the New England militiamen.

> We put no Confidence in any other Troops than theirs; and it is generally lamented that the British veterans were not put into Garrison and New England Irregulars sent to the Ohio. Their men fight from Principle and always succeed. The Behaviours of the New England Provincials at Albany is equally admirable and satisfactory. Instead of the Devastations committed by the [British regular] Troops in 1746, not a single Farmer has lost a Chicken or even a Mess of Herbs. They have five Chaplains and maintain the best Order in Camp. Public Prayers, Psalm-singing and Martial Exercises engrossed their whole Time at Albany. Twice a week they have Sermons and are in the very best frame of Mind for an Army, looking for success in a Dependence upon Almighty God . . . . Would to God the New England Disposition in this Respect were catching.[99]

The number of annual training days was fixed by law and varied considerably according to time and place. In 1631 the Massachusetts militia was so enthusiastic about training days that it mustered weekly. Within a year the enthusiasm waned and musters were then held monthly. By 1637 the interest had continued to decline and consequently drills were held only eight times a year. Subsequent changes in the law reduced the obligation to six times a year and then just four. Emergencies changed the militiamen's minds and prompted them to take muster more seriously. During King Philip's War the Massachusetts militia mustered every Sunday and one additional day per week.[100]

Training days became social occasions. Whole families attended. The women folk prepared the means which were taken in common. The children enjoyed a rare opportunity, at least in rural ar-

---

99 Extract of a letter from New York, dated 1 August, *The Public Advertiser*, 6 October 1755.
100 *Mass. Col. Rec.*, 1: 85, 90, 102, 124, 210; 4 part 1: 420; 5: 211-12.

eas, to socialize and to play with large numbers of other children. Many young, single men met their future wives at these gatherings. Occasionally, a church or public building had to be repaired and this was done as a part of, or adjunct to, training days.[101] A British officer described New England training under the watchful eye of five chaplains who assumed responsibility for the mortality and general decorum.[102]

To Jeffery Amherst's seasoned, professional officers the Americans were utterly ill-mannered and ungentlemanly. They ignored class distinctions which were all important among the British officer corps. They reported to Amherst that the officers joined their men in carousing and carrying on, often into the wee hours of the morning. The militia officers were as bad as the men, engaging in all manner of outrageous behavior. They often wore costumes and unacceptable, non-military clothing. Many officers failed to wear insignia or distinctive uniforms that would identify them amongst their men. Moreover, they failed to obey even the most rudimentary rules of sanitation. Men and officers alike stank for they failed to bathe or change and wash their clothing.[103]

---

101 "Training Day" in Thomas C. Cochran and Wayne Andrews, eds. *Concise Dictionary of American History.* Scribner's, 1962, 961.
102 *The Public Advertiser,* 6 October 1755.
103 *London Gazette,* September 1759. See also Jeffery Amherst Baron. *Commissary Wilson's Orderly Book: Expedition of the British and Provincial Army, Under Maj. Gen. Jeffrey Amherst, Against Ticonderoga and Crown Point, 1759.* No. 1. J. Munsell, 1857, p. 58.

The Colonial Massachusetts Militia

Those academics who were studying the founding period, roughly corresponding to the time in which the initial charter was operative, 1629-1684, focused their attention on civil and ecclesiastical affairs, rarely considering the militia. The trainbands appeared to them to have been less innovative than were the Puritan church and state. The scholars were looking for the innovations instituted by the leaders of Massachusetts Bay Colony in the meeting houses, not on the training fields. These investigators assumed that the Puritan founders departed from English institutional models solely to experiment with popular participation in the selection of civil and ecclesiastical leaders. By comparison, they chose to view the militia as a vestige of England, simply as a leftover from medieval times which had changed very little during the seventeenth century.[104]

In traditional studies, and in most secondary sources, the Massachusetts militia is viewed as a simple and logical extension of the colony, but unworthy of in-depth study because it was less innovative than most other aspects of American Puritan development. At most Massachusetts slightly modified the traditional English Puritan train band model as befitted the necessities of the new world. During the entirety of the Old Charter period of Massachusetts history, that is, 1629-1684, the colony struggled to define the precise limits on popular participation in government and church. The militia was drawn into this debate, perhaps reluctantly, as both actor and subject acted upon. We have discussed much of the origin of the Massachusetts militia above while discussing the general emergence of the New England Puritan militia.

The governor was commander-in-chief of the province. Direction of military affairs is naturally an executive function. He theoretically was required to lead troops in battle. He ordered the disposition of troops and alone decided what points to garrison. He could sound an alarm and call out the militia. He might be assisted by a Council of war, generally appointed by the General Court. Often militia officers served in the legislature and they brought with them an intimate knowledge of military situations in all parts of the province. By the end of Phips' term as governor the precedent was well established of

---

[104] Breen, T. H., "English Origins and New World Development: The Case of the Covenanted Militia in Seventeenth-Century Massachusetts," *Past & Present,* 57 (1972), pp. 74-96.

regarding various assistants, deputy and lieutenant governors, legislators and militia officers as an informal council of war.

The legislature retained the right to make the laws with respect to the militia and to fund the it. The General Court jealously guarded its prerogative to legislate in great detail concerning liability for service, arms required, inspection of arms and equipment, frequency of training and appointment, or at least confirmation, of officers. The legislature also created courts martial, prescribed punishment for various infractions and ensured subordination of the military to civilian authority. It supported the militia by offering bounties on Amerindian scalps when pressures on the frontier became too great. It also attempted to keep the frontier populated by forbidding desertion of frontier towns, primarily in order to retain a buffer between the unsettled frontier and the cities. Eventually, it allowed the colony's troops to assist other colonies. It also forbade the impressment of militiamen by force or trickery.[105]

Even before the first religious dissenters settled in Massachusetts, white adventurers had sacked Amerindian villages as far north as Maine. Some slave traders had raided the villages, taken some natives captive and sold them into the slave trade. Some villages along the coast, especially near Cape Cod, had already been deserted as the reputation of the ruthless traders grew. Many Amerindians had died of a plague a few years before the Pilgrims arrived in 1620, and this may account in some large measure for their inability to meet and expel the new wave of invaders. The Pilgrims were shocked to discover that Samoset greeted the first party to land in English.[106]

In 1626, in preparation for the voyage to populate what became the town of Boston, the founders prepared a list of military equipment which they considered indispensable to equip the projected 100 militiamen.

3 drums, to each 2 pairs of heads
2 ensignes
2 partizans, for captain and lieutenant
3 halberts
80 bastard musketts, with snaphaunces, 4 ffoot in the barrel
6 longe fowling pieces with bastard muskett boare, 6 ffoote longe

---
105 Spencer, Herbert Rusell. *Constitutional Conflict in Provincial Massachusetts.* Columbus, Ohio: Heer, 1905, ch. 7.
106 Senate Executive Document 95, 48th Congress, 2d Session, 38-39.

4 longe fowling pieces, with bastard muskett boare, 5.5 ffoote longe
10 ffull musketts, 4 ffoote barrel, with match-locks
90 bandoleers, for musketts, each with a bullett bagge
10 horne flaskes, for longe fowling pieces, each with a bullett bagge
100 swords and belts
60 corselets & 60 pikes; 20 half-pikes
12 bbls powder, 8 bbls for the forts; 4 for small shotte
8 pieces of land ordnance for the forts namely, 2 demie culverings, 30 c. weight a peace 3 sackers, each weighing 25 c. weight

The bandoleers were belts which each held 12 rounds of ammunition and a leather covered priming box. Ten bandoleers were of standard musket size and were stamped **M**, while two others were for bastard musket size and were stamped **B**. All bandoleers were purchased at pence each from John Grace of London. Twenty of the suits of armor were ordered from Thomas Stevens, Buttolph Lance, London. Armor consisted of corsalet, back, breast, culet, gorget, tases, and helmet, all varnished black. Four suits of armor were equipped with closed-visor helmets instead of the open type common to this period.[107]

In 1628 the General Court of Massachusetts created a fundamental charter which established political and legal authority in the colony, including power over the militia. The Charter recognized that safety and the peace could not be maintained without a well organized militia.[108] It observed that "Piety cannot be maintained without church ordinances and officers, nor justice without laws and magistrates, no more can our safety and peace be preserved without military orders and officers."[109] The "well ordered of the militia is a matter of great concernment to the safety and welfare of this commonwealth."[110] In 1628 John Endecott (c.1588-1655) emigrated to Massachusetts with sixty English colonists, joining those already at Salem. When the colony was properly organized he became, in 1630, the first head of the provincial militia. His expedition against the Pequots helped to

---

107 Peterson, Harold L. communication, in *The Gun Collector,* 4 (December 1946): 12

108 *Records of the Governor and Company of the Massachusetts Bay in New England.* N. B. Shurtleff, ed. State of Massachusetts, 1854, I, 17. Hereinafter cited as *Mass. Col. Rec.*

109 *Mass. Col. Rec.*, 1: 85.

110 The Charter and General Laws of the Colony and Province of Massachusetts Bay in *Mass. Col. Rec.*, 1: 157.

provoke the First Pequot War, which began in 1637. Between 1644 and his death on 15 March 1655 he served as governor.[111]

In the first report extant from Governor Cradock, dated 16 February 1629, the colony reported that it was attempting to spread Christian Gospel among the natives. Cradock reported considering enlisting friendly Christian Indians into the colony's militia. In its response to Cradock, dated 17 April 1629, the New England Company did nothing to encourage the military enlistment of natives, although it commended him on his attempt to convert them.[112]

The Charter of Massachusetts Bay of 1629 directed that the governor and company provide the inhabitants with "Armour, Weapons, Ordnance, Municon, Powder, Shott . . . and all Manner of Clothing, Implements, Furniture, Beastes, Cattle, Horses, mares, Marchandizes, and all other Thinges necessarie for the saide Plantacon and for their Use and Defence." The charter gave the governor the power to impose martial law, to build and maintain forts and other facilities and to maintain stores of arms and materials of war. More specifically, the charter required that the

> Governor of our said Province or Territory for the time being shall have full Power by himselfe or by any Chief Comander or other Officer or Officers to be appointed by him from time to time to traine, instruct, Exercise and Governe the Militia there and for the speciall Defence and safety of Our said Province or Territory to assemble in Martial Array and put in Warlike posture the Inhabitants of Our said Province or Territory and to lead and Conduct them and with them to Encounter, Expulse, Repell, Resist and pursue by force of Armes as well by sea as by Land within or without the limitts of Our said Province or Territory and alsoe to kill, slay, destroy and Conquer by all fitting wayes Enterprises and meanes whatsoever all and every such Person and Persons as shall at any time hereafter Attempt or Enterprize the destruccon, Invasion, Detriment or Annoyance of Our said Province or Territory . . . .[113][92]

In March 1631 the Court of Assistance of Massachusetts Bay ordered that all men, including indentured servants, but excluding magistrates and ministers, equip themselves with guns within two weeks. They were to have a minimum of 20 bullets, a length of match

---

111 Mayo, Laurence S. *John Endecott*. New York: DaCapo, 1971.
112 *Mass. Col. Rec.*, 1: 17, 384.
113 Poole, B. P., ed. *The Federal and State Constitutions, Colonial Charters and Other Organic Laws of the United States*. 2 vols. U. S. Government Printing Office, 1877, 1: 938-53.

a pound of gunpowder and other necessary accoutrements. If a man did not already own a gun the colony would advance him the money and he would have to pay it back within a reasonable time.[114] If a man could not pay for his gun the town would hire him, or hire him out to another man, until the cost of the gun was repaid. Farmers might pay for their arms in country produce.[115] No one was to travel, except within Boston, unless one was armed with a gun. Militia companies were all ordered to muster and drill on Sundays.[116] In 1632 the militia musters were reduced to just one every month[117]. The undated text of the first militia act of the colony of Massachusetts Bay read,

> Section 1. Forasmuch as the well ordering of the militia is a matter of great concernment to the safety and wellfare of this Commonwealth. It is ordered by this Court and the authority there of. . . .
>
> Section 9. Every person above the age of sixteen years shall duly attend all military exercises and service, as training, watching, warding under the penalty of five shillings for every fault, except magistrates, deputies and officers of court, elders and deacons, the president and fellows, students and officers of Harvard College, and professed school masters, physicians, chirourgeons allowed by the magistrates, treasurers, surveyor generals, public notary, masters of ships and other vessels above twenty tons, fishermen constantly employed at all fishing seasons, Constant herdsmen, and such other as, for bodily infirmity or other just cause shall by any County Court, or Court of Assistant (after notice of the partys desired to the chief officer of the Company to which he belongs) be discharged; also one servant of every magistrate and teaching elder, and the son and servant of the major general for the time being, also such as dwell at remote farms, shall be exempt from watching in the town, but shall watch and ward as their chief officer shall direct otherwise; and all farms distant above four miles from the place of exercising the Company, or have a ferry to pass over, that have about twenty acres of land in tillage, and twenty head of great cattle upon such farms, shall upon reasonable allowance to the Company, have one man exempted from ordinary trainings.[118]

---

114 In Daniel Boorstin, *Americans: The Colonial Experience*. Vintage, 1958, p. 355.
115 *Mass. Col. Rec.* 4: 222; 1: 93, 120.
116 *Mass. Col. Rec.*, 1: 85.
117 *Mass. Col. Rec.*, 1: 102.
118 *Characters and General Laws of the Colony and Provinces of Massachusetts Bay.* Boston: Prescott and Story, 1814, pp. 157-160.

The object of immediate concern for the militiamen of Massachusetts was the Pequot Indians. By 1635 the men of Massachusetts Bay were expanding rapidly into the distant Connecticut Valley and thus came into conflict with the indigenous land holders, the Pequots. When the Pequots killed seven of the interlopers, Massachusetts responded by mustering its militia, attacking the Pequots and killing several hundred of them. The survivors took refuge with other tribes. After this tribe was contained the colonial militia had to deal with the Narragansetts and their allies the Wampanoags, and the Abenakis and Penobscotts, allies of the French in Canada. The elitist Puritans had no trouble identifying the Amerindians as heathens and allies of the evil one. In turn the native Americans regarded the Puritans as unprincipled warriors who had no regard for their unwritten rules of conventional warfare. As the Chosen People, the Puritans thought they had an unbridled right to claim any territory they desired in their Promised Land.[119].

In 1635 the legislature ordered that militia fines be used to purchase arms for those too poor to provide their own guns.[120] On 9 September 1636 the provincial legislature voted to "limit ye election of Military Officers in ye several Towns to such only as are of ye trained bands and so thereby all such Freemen as are exempt from ordinary training should be barred from having any votes in such elections."[121] In 1636 officers elected by militia companies were still subject to legislative and executive approval.[122] Also in 1636 the colony of New Plymouth revised its law regarding indentured servants. One provision concerned the militia. "No servant coming out of his time or other single person be suffered to keep house," the law read, "till such time as he be completely provided for of arms and ammunition."[123]

In 1637 the legislature ordered that a long list of classes of persons accused of various ecclesiastical and civil offenses, including

---

119 Radabaugh, Jack S., "The Militia of Colonial Massachusetts," *Military Affairs*, 43 (1954), pp. 1-18; Howard H. Peckham, *The Colonial Wars, 1698-1762*. University of Chicago Press, 1964, 19-20.
120 *Mass. Col. Rec.*, 1: 137.
121 *Mass. Col. Rec.*, 2: 191.
122 *Mass. Col. Rec.*, 1: 187.
123 "Regulation of Servants in New Plymouth, 1636," in W. Keither Kavenagh, ed. *Foundations of Colonial America*. 3 vols. New York: Chelsea House, 1973, 1: 405.

blasphemy, religious heterodoxy, rape, sodomy and theft, "bee disarmed."[124] The apparent intention of the legislation was to deny arms to criminals and heretics because these were the symbol of freemen. On 24 April 1638 Governor John Winthrop incorporated the Military Company of Massachusetts, guaranteeing that "no officer should be put up[on them but of their own free choice." Each enlisted man was given 500 acres and each officer 1000 acres of land. The militia company was renamed the Ancient and Honorable Artillery Company on 2 September 1700.[125] In 1639 the legislature exempted from militia duty a number of classes of trades, including ships' carpenters, fishermen during season, and millers, but required them to maintain firearms.[126]

The community was the basic unit of many activities, including militia service. Towns were the basic units of military organization wherein men armed and trained themselves for war. Initially, all Boston area militias were rather democratic although the officers reflected the basic Calvinist hierarchy of church and state. All ablebodied males served in the militia, excepting certain governmental officials, but including indentured servants and slaves. The regiment was first noted in 1636 when Captain John Underhill brought the companies from Roxbury, Dorchester, Weymouth and Hingham under a single, unified command and integrated it with the South Boston Militia and other city militia companies. After 1637 men could nominate and elect their own officers from among the town's freemen, subject only to the (almost automatic) approval of town council.[127]

The average militiaman was little concerned about organization beyond his own company for it was in this basic unit that he socialized, trained, elected their own officers and fought when called into actual service. Most commoners were armed merely with pikes and some small cutting instrument, such as sword or scalping knives. A few of the wealthier citizens own match-locks and even fewer had wheel-locks. The companies marched out on the greens, often located convenient to the churches or town meeting houses, there to drill under the appreciative and watchful eyes of their families.

On 13 January 1639 the Ancient and Honorable Artillery Com-

---

124 *Mass. Col. Rec.*, 1: 212.
125 *Massachusetts Historical Society Collections,* Series 2, [1813], 2: 186-87.
126 *Mass. Col. Rec.*, 1: 258.
127 *Mass. Col. Rec.*, 1: 186-87.

pany of Boston was formed and the democratic pattern was broken. The militia unit was organized as an elitist organization, comprised exclusively of the prominent townsmen and was drawn largely from the harbor communities. To be accepted into this company was a certain indication that one had arrived socially. It emulated a similar elitist company in London and remained, throughout its history, largely self-regulating. John Winthrop was made an honorary colonel and first nominal commander.[128] It was the oldest company of artillery militia in the nation.

The men of Massachusetts were not always perfect citizens or part-time soldiers. Captain Underhill recorded that, upon sounding an alarm, he was amazed to see that his trained bands "knew not how to behave."[129] They often missed the legally mandated training days and failed to accept discipline or to maintain their arms in good working order. Those who failed to attend musters, maintain proper equipment and arms, or otherwise follow the militia law, paid fines which the town authorities put to good use buying flags and banners, drums and bugles and other impedimenta.

Towns served as vehicles for many forms of communal action. They performed what was then considered social welfare and engaged in various forms of social action. The principal function the town undertook was defense of home, citizen and community through the organization and maintenance of a militia. The militia also served a social function of social integration. To expedite their obligations, the town governments maintained watch-houses, supplies of gunpowder and flints and match, extra weapons and spare gun parts and armories, the latter often located in the basements of town meeting houses.

In 1634 Ensign Richard Morris entered into a political dispute with his commander and resigned his commission. In other cases, men displayed culpable, if not criminal, disregard for safety. In one incident in Watertown, a servant brought his loaded weapon to the training field. After going through the manual of arms and marching for a while with the loaded piece, he accidentally discharged it, wounding himself and three others. Captain Underhill noted that such

---

[128] *Mass. Col. Rec.* 1: 250; Darrell B. Rutman. *Winthrop's Boston.* University of North Carolina Press, 1965, pp. 215-16; Oliver A. Roberts. *History of the Military Company of Massachusetts, Now Called the Ancient and Honorable Artillery Company of Massachusetts, 1637-1888.* 4 volumes. Boston: Mudge, 1895.

[129] *Winthrop's Journal,* 1: 91-92.

carelessness with arms was not especially uncommon.[130]

The Pequot War was an armed conflict that took place in 1636 and ended in 1638 in New England, between the Pequot Amerindian tribe and the colonists from Massachusetts Bay, Plymouth, and Saybrook. The Pequot and the Mohegan people were once a single sociopolitical entity. They split into the two competing groups sometime before contact with the Puritan English colonists. After contact with Europeans the two groups picked different allies, the Pequot with the Dutch and the Mohegans with the English. The major difficulty arose over control of the lucrative fur trade. Following the murder of a fur trader, the clergy preached sermons suggesting making war, and the Massachusetts militia burned the villages to the ground and destroyed their crops so many starved in the following winter. The colonists received aid from allied from the Narragansett and Mohegan Amerindians. The colonists and their allies decisively defeated the Pequot, killing or taking prisoner about seven hundred Pequots. The victors sold the prisoners sold into slavery, shipping them to Bermuda or the West Indies, although some were claimed as salves by the allied Amerindians. The result was the elimination of the Pequot tribe as a viable entity and the colonial authorities classified the tribe as extinct.[131]

Wars served as a vehicle to obtain slaves and servants according to an order of the General Court in 1641. The law held there was to be no involuntary servitude, including "bond slavery, villeinage or captivity" in the colony "unless it be lawful captives taken in just wars."[132] In 1641 John Winthrop reported that a two-day training exercise had taken place in Boston, and that, "About 1200 men were exercised in most sorts of land service; yet it was observed that there w as no man drunk, though there w as plenty of wine and strong beer in the town, not an oath sworn, no quarrel, nor any hurt done."[133]

Despite the failures which made them easy targets for their critics, past and present, the militia performed major services. They

---

130 *Winthrop's Journal*, 1: 89-96.
131 Mason, John. *A Brief History of the Pequot War: Especially of the Memorable taking of their Fort at Mistick in Connecticut in 1637*. Boston: S. Kneeland & T. Green, 1736. See also Howard Bradstreet, *The Story of the War with the Pequots, Retold*. Yale University Press, 1933.
132 "General Order of Massachusetts, 1641," in Kavenagh, *Colonial America*, 1: 405.
133 Winthrop, John. *Winthrop's Journal*. 2 vols. James Kendal Hosmer, ed .2: 42.

served watch in the city wards and mounted the towers for seaward watch on Beacon Hill and at the Town Gate. Captain Underhill led the militia to the distant Connecticut frontier there to assist their neighbors in the Pequot Indian War. In 1642 the legislature received warning of the possibility of a major attack from Amerindians allied with the French. Militia training was increased.[134] The legislature took certain steps to close some gaps in the basic militia act. One amendment to the basic militia act required that even those who were not required to muster had to provide themselves with arms. "All persons exempt from training who yet are to find arms and are able to use them, shall appear with their compleat arms before the Military Commander twice in the year to bee exercised, . . . except physicians, church elders, scholars and surgeons."[135] The legislature also ordered "that every smith in this jurisdiction, laying aside all other business, do with all speed, attend the repairing of arms . . . of the several towns."[136]

In the same year the legislature moved to stem the trade in firearms, gunpowder and bullets to the Amerindians. The illegal arms trade had provided the natives with the wherewithal to massacre the settlers and defeat the militia. It noted that earlier legislation had failed to prevent arms from falling into the hands of the native aborigine. If any man was caught selling or bartering guns to the native aborigine he was to pay a fine of £10 for each firearm sold; £5 for each pound of gunpowder; and 40 shillings for each pound of lead, shot or bullets.[137] In 1640 the colony of New Plymouth had imposed a fine of £20 "upon any that shall give, trade, truck or exchange with the native Americans any kind of military arms, or guns of any length or sort whatsoever."[138]

In 1643 the General Court created a new provincial militia law. The preamble contained a strong endorsement of both morality and the value of a trained militia. "As piety cannot be maintained without church ordinances and officers, nor justice without laws and magistracy, no more can our safety and peace be preserved without

---

134 *Mass. Col. Rec.*, 2: 24, 25, 28, 29.
135 *Mass. Col. Rec.*, 2: 25.
136 *Mass. Col. Rec.*, 2: 25, 31.
137 *Mass. Col. Rec.*; "Laws of Massachusetts Relating to the Indians, 1642," in Kavenagh, *Colonial America*, 1: 413.
138 "Laws of New Plymouth, 5 March 1640," in Kavenagh, *Colonial America*, 1: 444

military orders and officers." Exemptions from the law were provided for students at Harvard College, schoolmasters, ministers of approved congregations, physicians, certain fishermen and magistrates. All other freemen were to muster four to six days a year for inspection and training. The Massachusetts militia was organized along county lines, the first provincial militia to be organized in this territorial manner. The county officers included a captain, one lieutenant, an ensign, three sergeants and three corporals. Initially, a company consisted of sixty-four men, but the number was eventually increased to one hundred. A new company could be formed anytime a unit of one hundred militiamen could be found.[139] The election of officers was provided for by law, but only a complete company was granted this right. This proved to be an effective incentive to maintain full company strength.[140]

> All persons of any Trayned Band, both freemen and others, who have taken the oath of residents, or shall take the same, and being no covenant servant in household with any other, shall have their votes in nomination of those persons who are to bee appointed captaines, or other inferior officers of the same band, provided they nominate none but such as shall be freemen.[141]

In 1643, following the failure of some militia officers and units in the Pequot War, the General Court set up an advisory committee on military preparedness that could also act decisively in emergencies. It was staffed primarily with county militia captains and other presumably learned men of war.[142] In 1643 the position of sergeant major general was established to oversee the m ilitary forces of the colony, and lieutenants were appointed to a s s is t him in each shire. Two years later the system was revised, the title of shire lieutenant was abandoned and sergeant majors were establish ed to command each shire regiment. These officers were to be elected by the "town soldiers of every town in each shire " and by the freemen of the town whether members of the trainbands or not. These officers served as long as they proved satisfactory to the General Court, and the only restriction on the choice of those eligible to vote was th at the nominees

---

139 *Mass. Col. Rec.*, 3: 267-68; 5: 16.
140 *Mass. Col. Rec.*, 3: 267-68.
141 *Mass. Col. Rec.*, 1: 188.
142 *Mass. Col. Rec.*, 2: 39, 42-43.

had to be freemen.[143]

In the 1640s and early 1650s the Massachusetts General Court began extending the military franchise. In 1643 the members of the legislature announced that the office of sergeant major general, the colony's highest military position, would be filled by the vote of the freemen. The freemen were given the right to select a sergeant major, who was the officer in charge of regimental affairs. Two years later the General Court decided that additional persons should be allowed to participate in the choice of sergeant majors, and it ordered that "not onely freemen but all that have taken the oath of fidelity, or shall take it before the election, (except servants or unsetled persons,) may have liberty of their votes."[144]

In 1644 the legislature passed legislation, not part of the militia act, which nonetheless had implications for that legislation. For reasons of personal safety and protection, "all inhabitants . . . are to have arms in their houses ready fixed for service." The legislature lamented the "neglect of ye arms of ye country" and ordered all inhabitants to have repaired all arms that were out of order. It also ordered the Surveyor General to import or otherwise obtain quality arms and to offered these arms at cost to all who might need decent guns.[145]

On 14 May 1645 the Massachusetts Assembly passed a law which required that all young men between the ages of ten and sixteen years practice with arms under the supervision of officers designated by the principal officers of the militia. These boys were the youngest being trained we have seen. They were to become skilled in the use of pikes, bows and arrows and guns. This pre-militia training was designed to make certain that all young men had adequate familiarity with the common militia weapons.[146]

The Assembly assumed that the citizenry would own its arms and would be familiar with the basic care and operation of these weapons. The annual inspection would ascertain which citizens had failed to provide weapons. The discipline would insure that each man would know where and how to form in case of emergency. Training time was set at eight days, with advance notice of six days.[147] In the

---
143 *Mass. Col. Rec.,* I: 75; 2:. 42, 117.
144 *Winthrop Papers,* 3: 503-4; 4: 106; *Mass. Col. Rec.,* 1: 221, 231.
145 *Mass. Col. Rec.,* 2: 67.
146 *Mass. Col. Rec.,* 1: 328.
147 "An Order about ye Choyce of Sergeant-majors and their Charge; the clarkes of bandes with their Charge & Oath & Military Watches," *Mass. Col. Rec.,* 3: 12.

earliest years one-third of a militia company was armed with pikes and the remainder with fire-locks. Pikes proved to be useless in deep woods combat and all men were soon equipped with fire-locks, but tomahawks, scalping knives and other edged weapons which were useful in hand-to-hand combat were added as standard equipment. "All inhabitants, seamen as well as others, are to have armes in their howses fitt for service, with pouder, bullets, match, as other souldiers; and ye fishermen, shipp carpenters & others not exempted by lawe shall watch . . . and traine twice a yeere according to order."[148]

The Assembly also ordered that the great militia be called out annually for minimal training. Companies were made up of sixty-four men. No company with less than a full roster of men was permitted to elect its own officers, a most important prerogative on the time and place. After the clerk certified to the General Court that a company had its required membership, the men "shall have liberty to choose sergeants and other inferior officers." These officers swore an oath to "trayne them in the use of armes, eight dayes in the yeere."[149]

The watch mandated in the law was designed principally to look for the approach of enemies from any direction. As a secondary function the watch was to look for crime in progress and to resist violence. If the watch came upon an enemy or criminal the men were to capture, or if necessary kill, the culprits. If their force was inadequate to contain the menace they were to fire warning shots to attract the attention of others. Citizens were expected to grab their own arms and rush to the assistance of the watchmen. Watch began "halfe an hower after sonne setting" and continued until dawn. Men were to be armed with muskets or pikes.[150]

The General Court also ordered "that all Scotsmen, Negers & Indians, inhabiting with or servants to the English, from the age of 16 to 60 yeares, shall be listed." These men were to be mustered, disciplined and trained with the rest of the company. Those who loved at such a distance as to be inconvenienced to travel to train with their companies were permitted to gather, if at least 12 in number, and train themselves six times a year; or to train with other companies if they lived close to another militia company than to their own.[151]

---

148 *Mass. Col. Rec.*, 1: 328; 2: 119.
149 *Mass. Col. Rec.*, 3: 267.
150 "Order of 18 June 1645," *Mass. Col. Rec.*, 3: 35-36.
151 *Mass. Col. Rec.,*, 3: 268.

In 1645 the legislature instituted two interesting changes of policy. First, the legislature ordered that musket and pistol balls were to be supplemented with swan shot.[152] Swan shot is commonly known in modern literature as buckshot and is used to discharge a relatively broad pattern, increasing the chances of even a poor marksman hitting his target in dense brush. Today it is used for hunting medium size game in urban areas because it does not carry nearly as far as a single ball. Muskets of the colonial period would have discharged about two ounces of shot pellets about the size of a pea. These shot could do considerable damage to man or even several men in a small group at ranges of fifty or more yards. The legislature also ordered that small children, those under the age of 16, were to acquaint themselves with arms. It suggested that children begin pre-induction militia training by practicing with scaled-down bows and arrows, small pikes and miniature guns.[153]

In May 1645 several of the colony's most important military officers requested permission from the General Court to create three private militia companies which would be similar to the one formed earlier in Boston. They would form these companies from towns in the counties of Essex, Middlesex, and Old Norfolk. The companies would determine their membership, elect their officers, and generally govern their own affairs. They would march, practice and drill "as often as they please." The stated goal of these organizations was to advancement the military arts and to carry out various social function as well. Governor Winthrop, was suspicious of granting any special military privileges, and thus disapproved of the plan. In his journal he noted that "the military officers prevailed with much importunity to have the whole power of those affairs committed to them; which was thought by divers of the court to be very unfit, and not so safe in times of peace; but a great part of the court being military officers, and others not willing to contend any further about it, the order passed, and the inconvenience whereof appeared soon after, and will more in future times."[154]

On 12 August 1645 the Assembly provided for the recruitment and special training of an elite corps. This select militia was to consist of the thirty best men from each of the larger militia units. Their

---

152 *Mass, Col. Rec.*, 2: 124.
153 *Mass. Col. Rec.*, 2: 12.
154 Winthrop, *History*, 1: 260; 2: 254. See also *Mass. Col. Rec.*, 2: 110-12.

training concentrated on tracking, capturing and expelling hostile Amerindians and the French woodsmen, the *coureur de bois*.[155] They were to be prepared to move against hostile elements within thirty minutes of receiving a call from the authorities. They were to keep their arms, powder, match and accoutrements fresh and ready.[156] The reference in the law to "fresh Match" tells us that they were armed with matchlock arms instead of flintlock or snaphaunce lock arms. These select militiamen were the forerunners of the Minute Men of fame at Lexington and Concord.

In 1647 the legislature made a number of changes to the militia act. The first alteration allowed those militiamen residing in the outlying areas to deduct their travel time to and from militia muster from the eight days they were required to serve annually.[157] Another new provision to the militia law that allowed "the militia officers of each Company . . . with the advise and consent of such soldiers as are allowed their Votes in Choice of their Officers, shall, from time to time, appoint days for training their companys, so that there shall be eight days appointed for the same every year."[158] Another amendment attempted to provide some standardization of arms. Henceforth, militiamen could not fulfill the obligation to provide arms with just any gun. "No musket shall be allowed for service under bastard musket bore and not under 3'9" in length, nor any piece above 4'3" and every soldier is to be furnished with [a] priming wire, worm and scourer, fitted to ye bore of his musket."[159] Finally, an additional law also made provision for armourers. "Upon any Military Expedition . . . all Smiths and other work Men are to attend the repairing of arms and other necessaries and may not refuse such pay as the Country affords."[160] In the same year the list of those exempted from militia service included: the students and faculty of Harvard; school masters; notary publics; physicians and surgeons; masters of ships at sea; millers; ferrymen; herdsmen and nearly all political and public officers. However, all except magistrates, physicians and teachers were

---

155 Coureurs de bois were independent entrepreneurial French Canadian traders who traveled in New France and the interior of North America, to trade with the native aborigine.
156 *Mass. Col. Rec.,* 2: 41.
157 *Mass. Col. Rec.* 2: 216.
158 *Mass. Col. Rec.* 2: 221.
159 *Mass. Col. Rec.* 2: 222.
160 *Mass. Col. Rec.* 2: 222.

to be provided with arms. The colony provided that those who could not afford arms were to be provided with them, but the poor may be required to perform public service or barter what they may have in excess to obtain the public arms.[161] On 20 May 1647 the legislature repealed the act of 9 September 1636 and allowed all freemen, and not just those required to attend militia musters, to vote on officers of the various militia companies.[162]

On 27 May 1652 the Massachusetts Assembly decided to expand the obligation to serve in the militia. Heretofore, Afro-Americans, whether freemen or slaves, were not enrolled in the militia. Amerindians who lived in peace with the colonists had also been exempted. The new act included "Negroes, Scotsmen and Indians living with, or in servitude to" the colonists were obliged to serve in the militia beginning at age 16 years. The inclusion of Scotsmen referred to indented captives, taken by Oliver Cromwell's forces at the Battle of Dunbar.[163] The General Court ordered that "all Scotsmen, Negroes and Indians inhabiting with, or servants to, the English" be mustered with the militia.[164] However, just five years later, the legislature passed a law which prohibited blacks, whether free or enslaved, and Amerindians from joining the militia in the interests of "the better ordering and settling of severall cases in the military companyes."[165]

By 1655 the colony had established minutemen and we find references to their training and deployment.[166] In 1656 the Assembly passed substantial new legislation relative to the militia. The amendments provided substantial penalties for avoidance of militia duty. Only those previously exempted and anyone exempted by the courts could escape the impact of the militia law.[167] The militia law was not all inclusive. As with the 1643 militia act, exceptions were made for the following: magistrates, court officers and their chief deputies, deacons of the Church, and the faculty and students at Harvard College. Certain civilians whose services were indispensable were exempted. These included ferrymen, millers, and fishermen and herdsmen who were permanently employed at their trades. Those frontiersmen who

---

161 *Mass. Col. Rec.* 2: 221.
162 *Mass. Col. Rec.* 3: 108.
163 *Mass. Col. Rec.* 2: 99; 3: 267-68, 397.
164 *Mass. Col. Rec.* 2: 99; 3: 268.
165 *Mass. Col. Rec.* 2: 397.
166 *Mass. Col. Rec.* 3: 41.
167 *Mass. Col. Rec.* 4: 257.

lived at too great a distance from a militia company to muster conveniently were also exempted. Smiths and carpenters, physicians and surgeons were exempted from regular service, but could be drafted when their special talents were needed. Naturally the disabled were exempt from militia service. The law made particular reference to the release of those who had a "natural or personal impediment" such as "want of years, greatness of age, defect of mind, failing of senses, or impotence of limbs." Those exempt from militia discipline still had to provide themselves with a musket.[168] No man might join the militia "but as are of honest and good report and freemen." Shortages of manpower caused the enlistment of men as young as sixteen years.[169]

In 1660 a new militia act required "every person above the age of sixteen years" to train except the usual civil and occupational list and "one servant of every magistrate and teaching elder, and the sons and servants of the Major General." No mention was made of Amerindians or persons of color. Additional training requirements were added, with specifics left to the military commanders.[170]

Initially, the colony had tried to fill all its militia obligations and requirements with volunteers and when this failed it had created a system of obligatory militia service.[171] The system which proved to be reasonable and durable was one of universal militia service supplemented with a secondary system of drafting militiamen to serve as artificers and garrison troops at forts.[172] The General Court placed great value in forts so a remarkable amount of the militiaman's time was spent in garrison duty in static fortifications.[173]

In ordinary times regiments were to drill once every three years, with the militia officers to work out the schedule.[174] The legislature then fixed specific dates between 1641 and 1651 and again between 1671 and 1676.[175] Some counties failed to muster their militia

---

168 *Mass. Col. Rec.* 1: 210, 258; 2: 221-22; 4, part 1: 14; 5: 51.
169 Shurtleff, Nathaniel B. and others, eds. *Records of the Colony of New Plymouth in New England.* 12 vols. Boston: State of Massachusetts, 1855-61, 2: 61.
170 *Manuscripts Archives of Massachusetts.*
171 *Mass. Col. Rec.* 5: 71, 76.
172 *Mass. Col. Rec.* 4, part 2: 575; 5: 48, 123, 144-45.
173 *Mass. Col. Rec.* 4, part 2, 332; 5: 73.
174 *Mass. Col. Rec.* 1: 158.
175 *Mass. Col. Rec.* 2: 256; 4, part 2: 486.

for regimental meetings and some general gatherings were devoted to other activities, such as repair of fixed fortifications.[176] The training paid off. In 1680 Jasper Danckaerts, who was unimpressed with the drill of the New York militia, complimented the military order and discipline he saw in Massachusetts.[177]

The General Court in 1665 decided that much "mischief" among the natives had been brought on by excessive drinking of alcoholic beverages so it prohibited absolutely the sale of any intoxicating substance to them. All the Indian trade was henceforth to be conducted in licensed trading houses. Finally, seeing that the natives had no sense of permanent conveyances of land, and that they became warlike when cheated out of their lands in order yo to satisfy debts to the traders, the Court forbade the sale of Indian land without its express approval.[178]

In 1668 the Massachusetts General Court yielded to internal and external pressures, and abolished local trainband elections altogether. It alone now claimed full authority to "nominate, choose, [and] appoint" commission officers. The freemen still selected a major general, the colony's highest ranking officer, but the non-freemen no longer possessed a voice in selecting most officers.[179]

In 1679 the General Court noted that "many people, both English and Indians that come to such [militia] meetings, as well as soldiers, commit many disorders of drunkenness, fighting and neglect of duty." Therefore, the legislature placed strict limitations on the sale and use of alcoholic beverages on training days. The General Court also instructed militiamen to lock up their weapons after training sessions had been concluded. It threatened dire punishment for those who "shall either singly or in companies remain in arms and vainly spend their time and powder by inordinate shooting in the day or night after their release."[180]

By 1687 it was evident that the colony had to enact an adequate militia law for its own protection. The gave assembly the reasons for creating the Militia Act of 1687. "Whereas it is absolutely

---

176 *Mass. Col. Rec.* 4, part 2: 276, 333.
177 *Journal of Jasper Danckaerts*. B. B. James and J. F. Jameson, eds. New York: Scribner's, 1913, pp. 239, 271.
178 *Mass. Col. Rec.* 4, part 2: 282; 5: 63.
179 *Mass. Col. Rec.,* 4 part 2, 368, 422.
180 *M ass. Col. Rec.*, 5: 211; *Massachusetts General Court, Charter and Laws.* Boston: 1814, p. 166.

necessary that the inhabitants throughout this Territory and Dominion be well armed and trained up in the art military, as well for the honour and service of his most excellent Majesty as for the preservation and defence thereof from any violence or invasion whatsoever, Be it therefore enacted by the Governour and Council and it is hereby enacted and ordained by the authority of the same . . . ." The law provided for universal free male public obligation to serve in the militia. The law provided, "That no person whatsoever above sixteen years of age remain unlisted. . . ." If the man could enlist himself, that was fine, but if not self-enrolled, the obligation fell upon "masters, mistresses, or employers, under the captain or other officers in the respective places of their abode . . . ." Men had the choice of serving in regiments of foot or horse. After a young man turned age sixteen he must enlist within "the space of six weeks, on penalty of forty shillings, and so for every six weeks such persons shall remain unlisted."[181]

Each man was responsible for obtaining and maintaining his own weapons, supplies and accoutrements. "And that every foot soldier be provided with a well-fixed musket, the barrel not under three foot in length and the bore for a bullet of twelve to the pound, a collar of bandoliers or cartouch box with twelve charges of powder and bullets at the least, and a sword, or, if the officer so appoint, with a good pike and sword . . . ." The militiamen had to present their arms and equipment on demand. He "so shall appear when and where appointed, upon penalty of six shillings for his default in not appearing and four shillings for want of each charge of powder or bullets, musket, pike, sword, bandoliers or cartouch box, so as the whole penalty for any person at one time exceed not ten shillings. . . ."[182]

The law provided that if a militiaman wanted to perform his service on horseback that the cavalryman also had to equip himself. As applied to cavalry, the law said "that every soldier belonging to the horse shall, when and where commanded, appear and be provided with a good serviceable horse covered with a good saddle, with holsters, breastplate and crupper, and case of good pistols and sword, and half a pound [of] powder, and twenty sizeable bullets, on penalty of

---

181 An Act for settling the Militia. Council Chamber in Boston, 24th of March, in the 4th year of the reign of our Sovereign Lord King James the second, Annoque Domini 1687. *Public Mass. Col. Rec.* 3: 429-33.
182 An Act for settling the Militia. Council Chamber in Boston, 24th of March, in the 4th year of the reign of our Sovereign Lord King James the second, Annoque Domini 1687. *Public Mass. Col. Rec.* 3: 429-33.

ten shillings for each time absence and six shillings for default of each the particulars above mentioned, so as the whole penalty for one time exceed not fifteen shillings." Even though the cavalryman had to provide his own pistols he still had to own a shoulder arm. "And every trooper [shall] have at his usual place of abode a well fixed carabine, with belt and swivel, on penalty of ten shillings, which they shall bring into the field when commanded, upon penalty of answering the same at a court martial."

Some militiamen might not be able to afford the required arms. There were some very poor families in early Massachusetts. Providing arms for several males, father and sons, placed a considerable burden on some families. The law,

> Provided nevertheless, that if any person who is to provide arms or ammunition cannot purchase them by such means as he hath, he shall bring to the clerk of the company so much corn or other merchantable goods as by apprizement of the clerk and two of the company mutually chosen by them shall be judged of a greater value by a fifth part than such arms and ammunition is of; and thereupon shall be excused from the penalty for want of arms and ammunition, but not from appearance, until he be provided for and furnished, which the said clerk shall do as soon as may be, by sale of such goods, and render the overplus if any be to the party. But if any person be not able to provide himself arms and ammunition, through his mere poverty, if he be single, he shall be put to service by any justice of the peace, to procure him estate to purchase arms with, and his master shall find him arms during his service; if otherwise, the selectmen, townsmen or overseers shall provide and furnish him with arms and ammunition at the publick charge of the town, the which arms shall be kept by the clerk of each respective company, well fixed and fitted for service, under the care and inspection of the chief military officers there.[183]

The law wished to provide local authorities with reliable and permanent militia company rosters. Therefore, any person wishing to move had to make the appropriate notification to his militia unit commander. "And it is further enacted by the authority aforesaid, That no person so listed as aforesaid shall depart thence without a discharge from the commander of the company or troop where listed, on penalty of forty shillings; and that no commander of any company or troop

---

183 An Act for settling the Militia. Council Chamber in Boston, 24th of March, in the 4th year of the reign of our Sovereign Lord King James the second, Annoque Domini 1687. *Public Mass. Col. Rec.* 3: 429-33.

shall refuse, when desired, to give a discharge in writing to any that is removing his abode out of the precincts, under the penalty of £5."

Proper equipment and uniforms were important to militia companies, partially to give the men a sense of pride in the units, and partially to assist in identifying the various units. "The Colonels of the respective Regiments, or other chief officers, shall once every year, at the least, issue out their warrants to their inferiour officers, commanding them to make diligent search and inquiry in their several precincts, that all be duly listed, armed and equipped, and to return to them such defects as shall be found, to the end the same may be reformed, on penalty of one hundred pounds."[184]

Flags and musical instruments were also extremely important to the militia units as they were to regular military units. Men marched to the beat of drums and both drums and trumpets conveyed orders and assignments. Flags identified various companies and served as a rallying point, especially after a battlefield was obscured by the haze produced by gunpowder. Thus, the law required that, "all Captains of companies of foot or troops of horse shall, within six months from and after publication of this act, provide for their companies and troops, drums, drummers and colours, trumpets, trumpeters and banners, at their own charge, under penalty of ten pounds, and so for every six months such commanders shall remain unprovided . . . ."[185]

Although custom and practice varied widely, in early Massachusetts various non-commissioned officers and important musicians were paid. "All trumpeters and drummers lately in service, or that shall by the several captains be put into that service, shall hold and attend the said service during the captain's pleasure, upon the salary of forty shillings per annum for a trumpeter and twenty shillings per annum for a drummer finding their trumpet and drum, and twenty shillings for a trumpeter and ten shillings for a drummer if the captain find them, upon penalty of forty shillings." If the militia fines were insufficient to provide the necessary equipment, town authorities had to find the funds to buy whatever was needed. The law provided that "in case the fines and forfeitures for defaults allowed to the captains as aforesaid shall fall short of the charge of providing drums, drummers and colours, the account thereof being given to the chief field of-

---

184 Ibid.
185 Ibid.

ficer and by him allowed, the sum wanting shall be supplied and satisfied by the select men, townsmen or overseers out of the moneys raised or to be raised to defray other public charge in each respective town."[186]

Officers were to drill, inspect, discipline and exercise their militia charges regularly. "And that three times in every year, or oftener if command be given by his Majesty's Captain General or Commander-in-chief for the time being, the several companies and troops in each Regiment shall meet at the next and most convenient place to be appointed by their respective officers, to be then and there by them mustered and exercised." Failure to exercise an officer's responsibilities could bring considerable penalties. "And it is further enacted by the authority aforesaid, That once every year, or oftener if thereunto commanded, each particular captain, or lieutenant, where no captain is appointed, shall give to his field officer, and the field officer to his Majesty's said Captain General or Commander-in-chief for the time being, fair written rolls of their respective companies and regiments. And if any field officer, captain or other inferiour officer or soldier shall neglect or contemn performing the lawful commands of their respective superiour officers, he or they shall be punished by fine, cashiering or other punishment, according to the discretion of a court martial."[187]

Men who failed to assume all their responsibilities, as we have seen, were subject to fines. The Militia Act provided for the disposition and distribution of militia fines. "That the several fines and forfeitures mentioned in this act and not declared in what manner they shall be recovered and how disposed of, that all such as do relate to any person under the degree of a captain shall be to the respective captains, to defray the charge of their companies or troops, and to be levied before the next exercising day, by distress and sale of the offender's goods, by the captain's warrant to the clerk; but if the offender be a servant the owner's goods shall be liable to the distress and sale as aforesaid so that satisfaction may be made: and for all other penalties mentioned in this act, the same shall be levied by distress and sale of the offender's goods and chattels, by warrant from the

---

186 An Act for settling the Militia. Council Chamber in Boston, 24th of March, in t the 4th year of the reign of our Sovereign Lord King James the second, Annoque Domini 1687. *Public Mass. Col. Rec.* 3: 429-33.
187 Ibid.

chief field officers in the respective places or from his Majesty's Captain General or Commander-in-chief for the time being; one half thereof shall be to our sovereign lord the King, his heirs and successors, for and toward the support of his government here, the other half to the informer."[188]

Standing watch was among the most unpopular duties a militiaman might draw, but, on the frontier and along the coast-line, it was among the most important duties to which he might be entrusted. When Amerindians might attack, or French or other hostile navies might land in wartime, watch duty was standard fare. Not surprisingly, the law provide, "That all persons listed as aforesaid shall readily attend and serve on the watch when appointed, under the penalty of three shillings for each default and that it shall and may be lawful for any captain or other commission officer under the degree of a captain, in their captain's absence, to grant warrants of distress against any persons whatsoever that shall absent themselves from their duty on the watch or night guards, they keeping an exact account of all sums and forfeitures levied and received thereby, which they are to render to their superiour officers when required: provided always, that no trooper shall be obliged to watch or ward but under the command of his proper officer, and in his proper arms."[189]

Firing arms was a standard method of issuing warnings and summoning aid. Spurious and random firing after nightfall were more than a minor inconvenience; they misled, even deceived an unsuspecting population. Thus, the act provided "that no person whatsoever presume to fire any small arms after eight of the clock at night, unless in case of an alarm, insurrection or other lawful occasion; and in either of the said cases, four muskets or small arms distinctly fired, or, where great guns are, the firing of one great gun and two muskets or small arms distinctly, and beating of drum, shall be taken for an alarm; and every person that shall neglect his duty in taking and giving forward any alarm by firing as aforesaid, or shall be guilty of firing any small arms after eight of the clock at night . . . ." The man engaging in the illicit or frivolous firing of arms "shall be fined or otherwise punished at the discretion of a court martial, not extending

---

188 An Act for settling the Militia. Council Chamber in Boston, 24th of March, in the 4th year of the reign of our Sovereign Lord King James the second, Annoque Domini 1687. *Public Mass. Col. Rec.* 3: 429-33.
189 Ibid.

to life or limb." Men were to assume that the firing of arms after sundown were call to arms and all militiamen must respond immediately. "And in case of such alarm, every soldier is immediately to repair armed to his colours or court of guard, upon the penalty of five pounds."[190]

The law also restricted the arbitrary discharge of large guns from ships in the harbor. "And for the better prevention of false alarms, that no captain, master or commander of any ship or vessel riding at anchor in any [of] the harbors, ports or bays within this Dominion, or any other person, fire any gun after eight of the clock at night, under penalty of forty shillings for every gun so fired, to be levied by warrant from the chief officer, not under the degree of a captain, (who is hereby impowered to administer an oath and give judgment thereupon,) by distress or sale of the offender's goods, or for want of distress the said chief officer is hereby impowered to commit such offender to jail, there to remain until payment of the same; and that in case the said officer shall not perform his duty therein, he shall forfeit ten pounds, to be levied by warrant from the Governor or Commander-in-chief for the time being: provided always, that this clause shall in no ways concern or extend to any captain or officer of any of his Majesty's ships of war, for their firing at setting of the watch."

There were exemptions from militia service. Naturally, professional and enlisted military officers and enlisted soldiers were exempted. Most others on the exemption list were civil officers, including, "all the members of his Majesty's council, justices of the peace, sheriffs, coroners, and all officers of courts; treasurers, surveyors and deputy surveyors; the clerks belonging to the surveyor's office; and one servant of every member of the council. . . .; as also all officers imployed about his Majesty's revenue." Also exempted were "ministers ; the president, fellows, students and officers of Harvard college; professors and allowed schoolmasters; physicians and chirurgeons [surgeons]; masters of ships and other vessels above twenty tons, in actual employ; constant fishermen and herdsmen."[191]

By the time the assembly had passed the Militia act of 1687, some militiamen had decided to question the right of government to

---

190 Ibid.
191 An Act for settling the Militia. Council Chamber in Boston, 24th of March, in the 4th year of the reign of our Sovereign Lord King James the second, Annoque Domini 1687. *Public Mass. Col. Rec.* 3: 429-33.

draft them for any service, and many refused to report for garrison and maintenance duties. Threatened by this near universal revolt the legislature provided for a method of escaping from the draft. One could hire a substitute for a minimal payment. Consequently, the real burden of serving unpleasant and boring duty details fell on the poorest citizens and the non-citizens, the unemployed, transients and freebooters. Men with certain skills, such as carpenters and smiths, were more liable for the draft than most militiamen simply because the work on fortifications required their services. One could also reduce one's chances of being drafted by contributing supplies and arms to the common cause.[192]

Militia officers in Massachusetts were popularly elected. Every soldier, as well as those exempted by the law from militia discipline, was allowed to participate in the election. Any freeman might stand for election. The troops having fewer than 64 members had officers appointed by the Assembly. The assembly encouraged smaller units to merge their troops, primarily to allow for the election of officers.[193] When there was a tie, or when more than one man was elected to a particular rank, the man with the greatest seniority in the militia was chosen as senior officer.[194] The Governor of the Colony or his designate served as the Major-General of the colonial militia. Officers might be required to present a certificate from their parsons, identifying them as part of the elect. The General Court was never pleased by the democratic selection process and after 1664 it increasingly meddled into the officer selection process, exercising its power to "nominate, choose and appoint" the militia officer class. Those wishing to serve as officers might petition the General Court, providing it with recommendations and testimonials relative to their alleged qualifications.[195] These papers were similar to those prepared for officers nominated democratically in earlier times. The Court still later chose to rotate militia officers with mixed results. After 1645 the General Court increasingly guarded its prerogative militia powers.[196] In October 1687, Governor Edmund Andros usurped the power to appoint all civil officers, including those of the provincial militia. His "despotic rule" continued through February 1689 when the people of

---

192 *Mass. Col. Rec.* 1: 212; 3: 368; 5: 48.
193 *Mass. Col. Rec.* 2: 221; 3: 42.
194 *Mass. Col. Rec.* 4: 106.
195 *Mass. Col. Rec.* 1: 117; 2: 124; 4, part 2: 368; 5: 69, 74.
196 *Mass. Col. Rec.* 2: 125; 4, part 2: 28, 74; 5: 80.

Boston, "as their contribution to the Glorious Revolution," removed him from authority.[197]

The sergeant major-general was the highest ranking militia officer in the colony. He could always replace officers in the field, an obvious military necessity when officers were killed, wounded or otherwise rendered incapable of serving. When the Sergeant Major-General of the militia called the unenrolled troops into service or into joint military training camps, he would decide the order of rank among the eligibles in each rank.[198] His own family was exempted from militia drill and assembly, and he received other privileges commensurate with his rank and importance. He or his designate negotiated with the officers of neighboring colonial militias.[199]

When the colony needed the services of the militia, a signal consisting of firing of four muskets, ringing of church bells or other pre-decided alarm, would call the assembly. Any man failing to respond was to be fined £5 sterling. Excepting a decision made by the Major-General, a local committee consisting of the officers of the militia units could decide to hold the militia or to dismiss it.[200]

Local officers, whether elected or appointed, had primary responsibilities for the organization and discipline of the militia companies. The county captain was the principal militia officer in each county. He was charged with inspecting the arms carried by militiamen and checking the people attending church or otherwise traveling to make certain that they were armed. At times the county militia units paid his salary from militia fines and at other times he General Court paid his stipend.[201] On occasion the General Court or Sergeant Major-General might send militia captains as emissaries to various Amerindian chiefs and villages. They might also act as mediators, negotiators or arbitrators in Amerindian affairs and disputes. They sometimes negotiated the release of Caucasian captives and hostages[202]

The sergeant-major assisted the county captain. He assessed fines, sought out delinquents, supervised drills and generally ordered

---

197 "Memoir of Roger Wolcott" [1759], in *Collections of the Connecticut Historical Society*, 3 [1861]: 321-36.
198 *Mass. Col. Rec.* 4: 56.
199 *Mass. Col. Rec.* 1: 160; 2: 268.
200 *Mass. Col. Rec.* 2: 43.
201 *Mass. Col. Rec.* 1: 99, 138, 160; 2: 38, 223.
202 *Mass. Col. Rec.* 2: 24; Radabaugh, "Massachusetts Militia," 7.

the company's military business. In times of crisis he led the forces and could, if necessary, impress goods into the public service.[203] The county militia clerk was assigned the most unpleasant tasks. So unpopular was the position that the General Court mandated that clerks serve when elected or appointed or pay a stiff fine. He called roll at militia musters and reported those who failed to attend. He also kept the equipment roster, noting any deficiencies and levying fines on those under-equipped and he made arrangements for the poor to work on public projects to pay for militia equipment that they could not afford.[204] He added various charges to the fines that were not paid immediately. In return he received one-quarter of all fines and generally received a kick-back or legal commission on purchases of supplies and equipment.[205]

The militia law required that each man supply himself with at least a pound of gunpowder and twenty bullets. If the gun was a firelock,[206] at least a foot of match rope must be supplied, and if a flintlock, spare flints were in order.[207] In addition militiamen usually carried a hatchet or tomahawk,[208] scalping knife or sword and knapsack and cartridge belt. The musket was considered the most effective weapon, and for a time attempts were made to provide them for all adult males. Economic difficulties and the supply factor precluded th is, and some men were allowed to substitute pikes as long as a ratio of tw o-thirds m usketeers to one-third pikemen was maintained. In any event, frequent inspections were held to insure that the required arms were available and serviceable, and fines were levied for any defects in equipment. Poverty was not deemed an acceptable excuse for fail-

---

203 *Mass. Col. Rec.* 2: 118, 256; 4, part 2: 28.
204 *Mass. Col. Rec.* 2: 222.
205 *Mass. Col. Rec.* 2: 118-19, 122; 3:9 398.
206 A firelock is a gun having a firing mechanism in which the priming is ignited by sparks struck from flint and steel, as the flintlock musket.
207 *Mass. Col. Rec.* 1: 85.
208 The origin of the word *tomahawk* is in dispute. A smith named Thomas Pearson who lived near Philadelphia in the late seventeenth century allegedly made an American improvement on the European hatchet, to be used as a weapon of war instead of a cutting instrument. Legend ascribes its origin to "Tommy Pearson." Webster's dictionary indicates that it was an adaptation of an Algonquin Indian word *tomehagen* or Mohican *tamoihecan* meaning a wooden war club. Later it was applied by the Amerindians to any and all war clubs or cutting instruments, iron or wood. Horace Edwin Hayden in *Pennsylvania Magazine of History and Biography,* 3 [1879]: 358.

ing to obey the law . Paupers were to be supplied with arms by the town m agistrates and then bound out as labor until the town .[209]

During the early decades, infusion of the martial spirit was deemed important, beginning at an early age. The authorities recommended that children from the ages of ten to sixteen years, at which time the men joined the militia, should be trained in the use of "small guns, half pikes, bows and arrows."[210]

Cavalry units were formed as auxiliaries to the regular militia. Initially, they served as scouts with infantry, but they rapidly developed into effective combat units.[211] First organized in units of thirty mounted men, cavalry units were expanded into units based on seventy men.[212] Units with forty or more mounted men could nominate their own officers.[213] These were the elite militiamen. Only freemen who were admitted to full citizenship, and, usually, were Puritans, could join the mounted militia. An applicant or his family had to own property valued at no less than £100 in order to serve in the cavalry. He had to equip himself with saddle, bridle, holster, pistol or carbine and sword and provide his own horse.[214] In return he received may privileges not accorded infantry militiamen. He could not be drafted, but had to volunteer, for service outside the colony. He paid no ferry charges or head rate poll tax.[215]

The General Court encouraged these militiamen living on or near the frontier in sparsely populated areas to develop mounted militia units to expedite muster and organizational time.[216] As long as the cavalry was properly utilized they proved to be effective. When they were misused and improperly deployed, as in King Philip's War, they suffered enormously and were nearly disbanded.[217] Frontiersmen usually valued their riding horses highly and were often unwilling to use their best horses in combat because of the possibility of injury. On the other hand, some militiamen were frequently guilty of overloading

---

209 General Court of Massachusetts, *Laws and Liberties.* Cambridge, 1647, p. 40; Mass. Col. Rec., I: 84-85, 125; 2: 43, 110, 222.
210 *Mass. Col. Rec.,* 2: 99.
211 *Mass. Col. Rec.* 4, part I: 379.
212 *Mass. Col. Rec.* 3: 265, 398.
213 *Mass. Col. Rec.* 1: 158, 164.
214 *Mass. Col. Rec.* 3: 264-65; 4, part 2, 97; 5: 438.
215 *Mass. Col. Rec.* 5: 49, 70-71, 4, part I: 323; 3: 398.
216 *Mass. Col. Rec.* 3: 419; 4, part 2: 439; 5: 254, 409-10.
217 *Mass. Col. Rec.* 5: 47, 70-71.

the horses so that the animals died en route to battles, or were so slower by the weight that they offered little advantage over foot soldiers.[218]

The Massachusetts Charter granted by William and Mary in 1691 read that the governor "shall have full Power by himselfe or by any Cheif Comander or other Officer or Officers to be appointed by him from time to time to traine instruct Exercise and Governe the Militia; there and for the speciall Defence and Safety of Our said Province or Territory to assemble in Martiall Array and put in Warlike posture the Inhabitants of Our said Province or Territory and to lead and Conduct them and with them to Encounter Expulse Repell Resist and pursue by force of forces by sea and hand with Armes. . . "[219]

Legislation enacted in 1692 gave the governor significant powers over the militia and over defense generally:

> Governour of our said Province or Territory for the time being, shall have full power by himself, or by any chief Commander, or other Officer or Officers, to be appointed by him from time to time, to Train, Instruct, Exercise and Govern the Militia, there; and for the special Defence and safety of our said Province or Territory, to Assemble in Martial Array, and put in Warlike Posture the Inhabitants of our said Province or Territory, and to Lead and Conduct them, and with them to Encounter, Expulse, Repel, Resist and Pursue by Force of Arms,* as well by Sea as by Land, within or without the Limits of our said Province or Territory, and also to kill, slay, destroy and conquer, by all fitting wayes, enterprizes and means whatsoever, all and every such Person and Persons as shall at any time hereafter attempt or enterprize the destruction, invasion, detriment or annoyance of our said Province or Territory; and to use and exercise the Law Martial in time of actual War, Invasion or Rebellion, as occasion shall necessarily require; and also from time to time to Erect Forts, and to Fortifie any Place or Places within our said Province or Territory, and the same to furnish with all necessary Ammunition, Provision and Stores of War, for offence or defence, and to commit from time to time, the Custody and Government of the same, to such person or persons as to him shall seem meet, and the said Forts and Fortifications to demolish at his pleasure. . .[220]

---

218 Mahon, John K., "Anglo-American Methods of Indian Warfare, 1676-1794," *Mississippi Valley Historical Review*, 15 [1958]: 254-75 at 256.

219 *The Acts and Resolves, Public and Private, of the Province of the Massachusetts Bay*, 1: 18.

220 Act of 8 June 1692 in Evans Early American Imprint Series.Boston. : Printed by Bartholomew Green, and John Allen, (printers to His Excellency the governour and Council,) for, and sold by Michael Perry at his shop over against the

On 2 July 1692 the legislature passed enacting legislation which allowed the militia to march to the relief of the neighboring provinces or colonies. It held that for as much as in this time of war there may be occasion for the raising of soldiers, and transporting or marching of them out of the limits of this province into the neighboring provinces and colonies of New Hampshire, Rhode Island, Connecticut, Narragansett, or New York for the prosecution of the French or Amerindian enemy and the defense of their majesties' subjects and interests.[221]

On 17 November 1692 the legislature enacted a militia act designed for the security of this their province against any violence or invasion what- ever, it is necessary that due care be taken that the inhabitants thereof be armed, trained, and in a suitable posture and readiness for the ends aforesaid, and that every person may know his duty and be obliged to perform the same."[222]

Town-House, and Benjamin Eliot under the west-end of the Town-House., 1699.
221 Chapter 8, Act of 2 June 1692 in *Acts and Resolves*, 1: 36, 99.
222 Chapter 3. An Act for Regulating of the Militia; 17 November 1692. *Acts and Resolves*, 1: 128.

King Philip's War

The Wampanoag tribe has been peaceful, even friendly, toward the European settlers under Massasoit, and there were few problems as long as he lived. On Massasoit's death in 1661 he was briefly followed by his elder son Alexander. Upon Alexander's death King Philip, Massasoit's second son, became the sachem of the Wampanoags. A proud and talented, even charismatic, but brooding, man, King Philip had long envied the physical possessions of the Europeans and loathed their encroachment on the Wampanoag's ancestral lands. He mourned the passing of tribal autonomy and independence, especially with their growing dependence, even addition, to the white man's goods. He thought that he was to be joined by the Narragansett tribe of Rhode Island, which resented what they considered preferential treatment of the rival Mohican tribe. The Narragansett and Wampanoag tribes, traditional enemies, had found new reasons to bury the hatchet. King Philip's War began in June 1675 when Wampanoag warriors attached and destroyed the frontier town of Swansea, thirty miles form Plymouth. Plymouth Plantation and Massachusetts militiamen hurried to the scene. The Narrgansetts watched and waited and while the Mohican and Pequot tribes assisted the colonists.

The Amerindian tribes which lived in New England typically had a love-hate relationship with the European colonists. The Pequot nation, which lived chiefly in eastern Connecticut, was the first tribe to be subdued by the local militia. Following that war, the Narragansetts, who became allies of King Philip of the Wampanoags, became the principal obstacle to colonial expansion. The native aborigine of Rhode Island were never a match for either the colonists or the more aggressive tribe to their north, namely the Abenakis and the Penobscots. The latter were Canadian tribes, allies of the French, and constantly hostile to the colonials.[223]

King Philip's War is also known as the First Amerindian War, the Great Narragansett War and Metacom's Rebellion. Action occurred in southern New England from 1675 to 1676 and was the last-ditch effort by the native aborigine to avoid falling completely under English authority. Philip (Metacom), sachem [chief)] of the Wampanoag tribe, was a son of Massasoit, who had greeted the first

---

223 Radabaugh, Jack S., "The Militia of Colonial Massachusetts," *Military Affairs,* 18: 1 (1954), pp. 1-18.

colonists of New England at Plymouth in 1621. The Amerindians hoped to end continual English settlement on their lands. The war was named after the Wampanoag chief Metacom, who is generally known in history as King Philip.[224]

In January 1675, a Christian Amerindian convert named John Sassamon warned Plymouth Colony about Philip's impending attack upon English settlements. John Sassamon was a Harvard-educated convert to Puritanism, which converts were known as praying Indians. Sassamon had served as an interpreter and advisor to Philip but Philip had accused him of spying for the colonists. He played a key role as a cultural mediator, negotiating with both colonists and Natives while belonging to neither party. The colonists ignored this warning. Soon after issuing the warning the colonials came upon Sassamon's murdered body in an icy pond. The colonists then took action. They accused Philip of plotting Sassamon's murder. A jury made up of colonists and Amerindians found three Wampanoag men guilty of Sassamon's murder and hanged them on 8 June 1675. Their execution incensed Philip, setting the stage for war.[225]

King Philip's War began when the Wampanoag attacked Swansea and ambushed an English relief column. Between 20 June 20 and 23 June 1675, the Wampanoag carried out a series of raids against the Swansea colony of Massachusetts, killing many colonists and pillaging and destroying property. Colonial officials responded by sending their militia to destroy Philip's home village of Mount Hope, Rhode Island.

Having established generally good relations with the local Amerindians, political authorities in Rhode Island wished to remain neutral during this conflict known as King Philip's War. However, the Rhode Island General Assembly had no choice but to allow the militias from Massachusetts and Connecticut to march through its territory, as these units moved against the natives. Consequently, Rhode Island became the epicenter of this bloody struggle. King Phillip's War had begun as a conflict between Plymouth colony and the Wampanoag Amerindian tribe, but quickly spread to Rhode Island. Initially, public officers in Rhode Island officials attempted to arbi-

---

224 Brooks, Lisa. *Our Beloved Kin: A New History of King Philip's War.* Yale University Press, 2019, ch. 1.

225 Kawashima, Yasuhide. *Igniting King Philip's War: The John Sassamon Murder Trial.* University Press of Kansas, 2001.

trate an end to the Plymouth and Wampanoag conflict. However, Governor William Coddington violated the neutrality by aiding Plymouth by providing vessels to assist in the capture of Metacomet, the son of Massasoit and chief of the Wampanoag whom the colonists called Philip.[226]

Because of the New England Confederation, which had been created on 19 May 1643, following the disasters of the Pequot War (1636-1637), Plymouth, Massachusetts Bay, Connecticut and New Haven had a military alliance in place. Those colonies had prepared certain war plans and were therefore at least partially prepared to defend against their common enemies. Rhode Island was not a participant and apparently was never invited to join. Over the subsequent years, the New England Confederation occasionally clashed with the Wampanoag, Nipmuck, Pocumtuck and Narragansett Amerindian tribes, which kept the New England Confederation prepared. Rhoide Island had made no preparations for either a war against the natives or full military cooperation with its neighboring provinces.[227]

In July 1675, the Massachusetts militia under Captain Benjamin Church trapped King Philip in a swamp near Pocasset. Church decided to starve the Amerindians into submission. He discharged many of the militiamen. Philip, noting the depleted numbers of militiamen, managed to slip away, fleeing to Nipmuck's territory. During the pursuit Church's militia united with a group of Providence militia, commanded by Captain Andrew Edmonds. On the first of August the combined militia companies tangled with King Philip's warriors in an indecisive battle.[228]

On 9 September 1675, the New England Confederation declared war against King Philip and his followers. A week later, approximately seven hundred Nipmuc Amerindians ambushed a militia patrol which was escorting a wagon train of colonists. The warriors killed and scalped nearly all the colonists and the militiamen. This engagement is known as the Battle of Bloody Brook.

By October 1675 town officials in Providence had become concerned about possible raids. On 14 October they decided to post sentinels and mount patrols. Many settlers deserted the town. On 27

---

226 James, Sydney V. *Colonial Rhode Island: A History.* Scribner's, 1975, p. 93.
227 Mandell, Daniel R. *King Philip's War: Colonial Expansion, Native Resistance, and the End of Indian Sovereignty.* Johns Hopkins University Press, 2010.
228 James, *op. cit.,* pp. 93-94.

March 1676, the Narragansett leader Chief Canonchet led his warriors against the town. There was no militia force available that might have restrained the attack. Roger Williams and twenty-seven men took refuge in a fortified house. Williams then attempted to negotiate a peaceful solution. Reportedly, Canonchet vowed he would not harm Williams because Williams was a good man. Nonetheless, the Amerindians burned much of Providence.[229] Despite the deployment of approximately eleven hundred New England militiamen, the end result was the abandonment of most Rhode Island settlements led to the burning and destruction of Smith's Trading post, Warwick, and Providence.

If the reasons for maintenance of a colonial militia were not obvious heretofore there occurred the most disastrous and horrific war New England was ever to know. Other raids struck near Taunton, Tiverton, and Dartmouth. Despite being forewarned and their advantage in numbers, the English were in serious trouble. The Amerindians were well-armed with firearms. While some came from the French, the Amerindians acquired most guns through trade with the English themselves. The Wampanoag and their allies even had their own forges and gunsmiths. Drawing from virtually every tribe in New England, Philip commanded more than a thousand warriors, and even the tribes who chose to remain neutral were often willing to provide food and shelter. Only the Mohegan tribe under Oneko, son of Uncas, remained loyal to the English. Particularly disturbing to the colonists was the defection of most of the "Praying Indians."

In 1675 in the midst of the war the colonial government admitted that it was having difficulty collecting adequate information about potential officers, and it asked the town militia committees to recommend "useful & fitt persons for that service." Members of the General Court who appointed the militia officers began to solicit the opinion of their fellow citizens as to names of those suitable to serve as militia officers.[230]

Although the Narragansetts had attempted to stay neutral, individual Narragansett warriors had participated clandestinely in raids on colonial strongholds and towns. The militia at first avoided clashing with the Narragansetts. Eventually, colonial leaders judged the Narra-

---

229 James, *op. cit.*, pp. 404-413. See also William G. McLoughlin, *Rhode Island: A Bicentennial History*. Norton, 1978, pp. 43-44.
230 *Mass. Col. Rec.*, 5: 30.

gansetts to be in violation of a series of peace treaties, leading the United Colonies of Massachusetts Bay, Plymouth, and Connecticut to amass the largest colonial army assembled to date in New England, consisting of at least a thousand militiamen and approximately one hundred and fifty Amerindian allies. In November 1675 Governor Josiah Winslow of Plymouth Colony gathered the colonial militia in Rhode Island territory. Their objective was to attack the Narragansett before they could mount a spring offensive.

    The militia immediately gained the upper hand. They drove Philip from the Mount Hope Peninsula and trapped them in a dismal swamp. The militia was too poorly led and disciplined to close the trap and Philip escaped, enlisting the Nipmuck tribe of central Massachusetts during his escape. In December 1675 the militia made a second mistake. Unable to get the Narraganset to make any clear statement of commitment they moved against their principal fortified town. This settled the issue and, with the Narragansetts now among the belligerents, other tribes joined the war. One tribe or another pillaged nearly every small frontier town and outlying farm. Finally, Brookfield was destroyed. They laid waste the Connecticut Valley. Militia sent in pursuit of raiders frequently fell victim to ambushes.

    The colonial militia, consisting of men from the colonies of Massachusetts, Plymouth and Connecticut, attacked a massive Narragansett and Wampanoag fortification near the Great Swamp in West Kingston, Rhode Island, on the morning of 19 December, during a bitterly cold snow storm. Captain Andrew Edmonds led the Providence militia at this crucial juncture.[231] The militia and its native allies began their attack on the Narragansetts' main fort, situated on an island amid a frozen swamp in what is now West Kingston, Rhode Island.

    During the Great Swamp Fight on 19 December, Colonel Benjamin Church, the ranger leader, was wounded while serving as an aide to Governor Winslow, the commander of the colonial forces in the battle. Governor Winslow had permitted Church to recruit Native Americans after he and other militia leaders realized that traditional European military tactics were ineffective in frontier warfare. Church's men were the first colonial force to be successful in raiding the hostile Indians' camps in forests and swamps. This earlier form of warfare was in some respects far more brutal and devastating than what came later; but the tendency to blur the differences between

---

231 McLoughlin, *Rhode Island,* p. 43.

civilians and combatants has remained a troubling part of our martial heritage. During previous decades, colonists had been on the defense against the native aborigine, who knew their territory intimately. It relied upon unconventional methods, and could be terrifyingly violent. This became a distinctive American frontier form of warfare, much related to *la petite guerre.*[232]

Colonel Church also persuaded many neutral or formerly hostile Indians to surrender and join his unit, where they operated skillfully as irregular troops. Some of these men had converted to Christianity in settlements before the war. They were known as Praying Indians. After being organized by Church, these troops tracked hostile Indians into the forests and swamps, and conducted effective raids and ambushes on their camps. Perhaps three hundred Amerindians, including women and children, were either killed in the attack or subsequently died from exposure. Reportedly, some natives were burned alive at the stake.[233]

Philip retreated following the Great Swamp Fight, establishing his camp in New York. However, the Mohawk, friendly with the British, attacked the Wampanoag and forced them to retreat to New England. After the Great Swamp Fight, Church and the colonial army were 15 miles from their base in North Kingstown and had to endure a long march encumbered by dragging their dead and wounded and severe cold.[234]

During the winter of 1675-1676, King Philip continued to attack the colonies throughout New England. Philip's warriors attacked Plymouth Plantation, forcing colonists to flee to the coast. Another marauding band led by Chief Canonchet, totally annihilated Providence, Rhode Island. In another attack, known as the "Nine Men's Misery," Narragansett braves ambushed some sixty or so colonists along with twenty Christian Wampanoag Amerindians. They massacred most of the colonists, but chose nine men to be gruesomely tortured to death.

---

232 Grenier, John. *The First Way of War: American War Making on the Frontier.* Cambridge University Press. 2005, pp. 32-35.

233 Church, Benjamin, as told to Thomas Church. *The History of Philip's War, Commonly Called The Great Indian War of 1675 and 1676.* Samuel G. Drake, ed. Exeter, NH: J & B Williams, 1829. Facsimile Reprint by Heritage Books, 1989.

234 Zelner, Kyle F. *A Rabble in Arms: Massachusetts Towns and Militiamen during King Philip's War.* New York University Press, 2009.

On 10 February 1676 the Amerindians burned Lancaster and eleven days later destroyed much of Medfield. On 13 March they successfully attached Groton, which was burned after it inhabitants fled. Providence and Warwick, Rhode Island, and Simsbury, Connecticut, were abandoned. The Massachusetts towns of Andover, Woburn, Sudbury, Bridgewater, Hadley, Hatfield, Springfield and Marlboro were all successfully attacked. Urban areas had to provide for increasingly large numbers of refugees and prices of foodstuff rose as crops were burned and cattle and horses slaughtered in the fields. But the militia was learning the military supplies arrived from England. The Amerindians had no outside sources of supply and no sense of planning for a prolonged war. Militia had burned their crops and killed many of best warriors. Hunger, malnutrition and disease took horrible tolls.

When Puritan missionaries attempted to gather their converts, only five hundred could be found. The others had either taken to the woods or joined Philip. Their loyalty still suspect, the Praying Indians who remained were sent to the islands of Boston Harbor. In March Canonchet and the Narragansett almost wiped out one command, killing sixty men, and in another fight shortly afterward killed seventy more. With these successes Philip was able to gather a large number of warriors at Squawkeag, but he was unable to feed them. Although he was able to raid the English with impunity and fend off the Mohawk, Philip desperately needed to clear English settlement from the area so his people could plant corn and feed themselves. For this reason, the Narragansett and Pocumtuc joined forces in attacks on Northfield and Deerfield during the spring of 1676. Both raids were ultimately repulsed with heavy losses to both sides.[235]

Meanwhile, Philip's followers needed seed corn for spring planting. Canonchet volunteered in April for the dangerous task of returning to Rhode Island where the Narragansett had a secret cache. He succeeded, but on the return journey was captured and executed by the Mohegan. Canonchet's death seemed to dishearten Philip and marked the turning point of the war. Philip moved his headquarters to Mount Wachusett, but the English had finally begun to utilize Praying Indians as scouts and became more effective. In May Captain

---

235 Schultz, Eric B.; and Michael J. Tougias. *King Philip's War: The History and Legacy of America's Forgotten Conflict.* W. W. Norton, 2000. We have followed this work closely in our description of the vents of King Philip's War.

William Turner attacked a fishing camp at Turner's Falls killing over four hundred of Philip's followers. Before forced to retreat by superior numbers, the English also killed several gunsmiths and destroyed Philip's forges. Turner lost forty-three men on his retreat to Hatfield, but the damage had been done. Philip's confederacy began to disintegrate.[236]

By 1676, the Amerindian population had decreased to about ten thousand, largely because of diseases. These numbers included about four thousand Narragansetts of western Rhode Island and eastern Connecticut; twenty-four hundred Nipmucs who lived in central and western Massachusetts, and approximately the same number in the combined Massachusetts and Pawtucket tribes which inhabited Massachusetts Bay, extending northwest to Maine. The Wampanoags and Pokanokets of Plymouth and eastern Rhode Island numbered fewer than a thousand inhabitants.[237]

By the spring of 1676, the tide began to turn in favor of the colonists. In April, colonial militiamen captured Chief Canonchet and turned him over to the Mohegans who shot, beheaded and quartered him. This left the Narragansetts leaderless. In May, militia attacked and killed as many as two hundred Narragansett warriors at the Battle of Turner Falls at Peskeompscut near the Connecticut River.

On 2 July 1676 a major engagement took place known as the Battle of Nipsachuck. It is noteworthy if only because it included a rare deployment of a cavalry charge instigated by English colonists. In the summer of 1676, a band of over a hundred Narragansetts were being led by female sachem named Quaiapen. This band returned to northern Rhode Island, apparently seeking to recover obtain seed corn for planting. A force of three hundred Connecticut militiamen, supported by approximately Mohegan and Pequot warriors, intercepted the Narragansetts. They killed Quaiapen along with other leaders as they retreated into the Mattekonnit Swamp near North Smithfield. Those who were not killed were sold into slavery.[238]

Metacomet took refuge at Assawompset Pond, an Wampanoag settlement, but the colonists formed raiding parties with indigenous

---

236 Brooks, Lisa. *Our Beloved Kin: A New History of King Philip's War*. Yale University Press, 2019.
237 Osgood, Herbert L. *The American Colonies in the Seventeenth Century* (1904). 2 vols. Forgotten Books reprint, 2010, 1: 543. We have found no better estimate.
238 Leach, Douglas Edward. *Flintlock and Tomahawk: New England in King Philip's War* (1954). Parnassus Imprints reprint, 1992, pp. 200-03.

allies, and he retreated southwest towards Rhode Island. One of the militia companies from Plymouth Colony led by Captains Benjamin Church and Josiah Standish tracked Metacomet to Mount Hope in Bristol, Rhode Island, where he was shot and killed on 12 August 1676. They beheaded Metacomet's corpse and his head was displayed in Plymouth for a generation.[239] The war dragged on with sporadic attacks as late as the summer of 1677 in Maine. In a most unconventional tactic for the Amerindians, the Pequots made their last stand in a fort near present-day Mystic, Connecticut, as did the Wampanog allies of King Philip on Rhode Island.[240]

Phillip's chief advisor Pumham was captured in Dedham on 25 July 1676. Pumham was so badly wounded that he could barely stand, but he grabbed hold of a militiaman and would have killed him had not one of the man's compatriots come to his rescue. An English-Amerindian militiaman named John Alderman shot and killed King Philip on 20 August 1676, at Mount Hope. Victorious militiamen then hung up his body, beheaded it, and drew and quartered it. They returned with Philip's head to Plymouth colony where it was displayed for years after. This assassination effectively ended King Philip's War although some minor engagements continued throughout New England until the Treaty of Casco was signed in 1678. While the Treaty of Casco is quite important because it brought to a close the war between the eastern Amerindians and English settlers, there exists no surviving copy of the treaty.[241] The Pokanoket tribe was prevented from signing the Treaty of Casco because of an E bounty which colonial officials had placed on the lives of every Pokanoket over the age fourteen.[242]

King Philip's War in New England by and large ended with Metacomet's death. More than a thousand colonists and three thou-

---

[239] Schultz and Tougias, *op. cit.*, p. 290.
[240] The outline of the war is taken from the best book on this subject, Douglas Leach. *Flintlock and Tomahawk: New England in King Philip's War.* New York: Macmillan, 1958. See also George M. Bodge. *Soldiers in King Philip's War* Boston: third ed.; Little Brown, 1906; Benjamin F. Stevens. *King Philip's War.* Boston: Sawyer, 1900; and Douglas Leach, ed. *A Rhode Islander Reports on King Philip's War.* Providence, R. I.: Brown University Press 1963.
[241] What is known of the treaty was derived from a summary in Jeremy Belknap, *The History of New-Hampshire.* 2 vols. Philadelphia: Robert Aitken, 1784, 1:158–59
[242] *Proceedings of the Massachusetts Historical Society,* 13 (1873–5), p.341

sand native aborigine had been killed or starved.[243] Amerindians attacked more than half of all New England towns and several were completely destroyed. The colonists, through the use of their militia, enslaved hundreds of the aboriginal captives. While some women and children were condemned to serve as slaves to the households of English settlers, the majority were transported to slave markets in Bermuda, Barbados, Jamaica, Spain, Portugal, Madeira, and the Azores.[244] This effectively eliminated the Amerindians as adversaries.

The war had devastated the Colony of Rhode Island. Its principal city, Providence, had been utterly destroyed. For its part, the Rhode Island legislature issued a formal rebuke to Connecticut Governor John Winthrop on October 26, although Winthrop had already died. This "official letter" placed the blame squarely on the United Colonies of New England for causing the war by provoking the Narragansetts.[245]

As the war entered its final phases, the colonists began to offer amnesty to many of their enemies. Colonial officials also offered bounties on warring aborigine. As a result of the bounty, the some Pokanokets and other former allies of King Philip fled. Many were executed or forced to sign contracts of indentured servitude, and the survivors went into hiding, identifying themselves by using the general term Wampanoag, which included dozens of tribes. Some of Philip's original allies fled North to continue their fight against the colonists.

A recent study of the Rhode Island militia concluded that the destruction of the mainland settlements during King Phillip's War ensured that the Rhode Island General Assembly maintained the freedom to raise and employ men for defense, as they deemed appropriate while maintaining a strong sense of community with the other New England colonies.[246] Given the tiny population of Rhode Island, such inter-re-

---

243 Other estimates suggest that as many as two thousand Amerindians were killed and another three thousand starved or died of various war-induced illnesses. Nathaniel Philbrick. *Mayflower: A Story of Courage, Community, and War.* Penguin, 2006, p. 332.

244 Peterson, Mark A. *The City-State of Boston: The Rise and Fall of an Atlantic Power, 1630–1865.* Princeton University Press. 2019, pp. 129–131.

245 Cited in Allen, Zachariah. *Bi-centenary of the Burning of Providence in 1676: Defence of the Rhode Island System of Treatment of the Indians, and of Civil and Religious Liberty. An Address Delivered Before the Rhode Island Historical Society.* Providence Press Company, 10 April 1876. pp. 11–12.

246 York, *op. cit.*, p. 26.

gional cooperation was a matter of absolute necessity.

During King Phillip's War Rhode Island militiamen had acted independently of the Assembly'decision to remain neutral. These men had volunteered to assist the Massachusetts and Connecticut militias operating in Rhode Island for the sole reason of protecting and defending their homes. This volunteer tradition continued, and even expanded, during the French and Indian War.

Colonial militia leaders had learned some expensive lessons. They saw the value of hiring other Indians to track and scout. They changed their principal weapons. King Philip's War marked the end of the European pike as a principal militia weapon in American. Amerindians were much more intimidated by the thunder and novelty of firearms than they were by pikes creating light infantry and of abandoning obsolete and useless equipment and accoutrements which added nothing and only burdened the militia-man.[247] They learned to make war in Amerindian fashion in the deep woods. A few months of actual service proved to be infinitely more useful than years of militia muster and marching. It was King's Philip's war that changed the American militia from a European para-military organization into an Indian fighting machine.[248] The American Revolution would force the militia to reverse that pattern.

Much has been written of the barbarous behavior of the Amerindians during King Philip's War, but little has been written of the devastating effect it had on the natives. The New England militia had realized that, if properly armed, equipped, united and led, the natives just might win the war. The Christian natives, derisively called "Praying Indians," represented an enormous reservoir of strength if Philip could rally them to his cause. Many of the converts owned firearms, some had money and supplies, most knew the whites and their battle tactics well, and many were sympathetic to at least some of Philip's causes. Some Caucasian leaders thought that the converts were not to be trusted, and it was just a matter of time before they joined Philip. They were almost certain to spy on the whites and report weaknesses in deployment of troops and fortifications that Philip could exploit. One preacher summed up this opinion: "We have been nourishing vipers." While standing firm against this opinion initially,

---

247 *Mass. Col. Rec.* 2: 43; V, 47.
248 See Harold Peterson, "The Military Equipment of the Plymouth and Bay Colonies, 1620-1690," *New England Quarterly*, 20 (1947), pp. 197-208.

to the point of defending the Christian Indians, the magistrates saw their authority undermined, and their position eroded, as a few cases of treason and spying were uncovered. So the praying Indians were murdered, their property confiscated, and their buildings burned and cattle killed. More converts defected and joined Philip, precipitating more reprisals. By the time the dreadful war was over perhaps as many as three thousand supposedly friendly Indians had been murdered, scattered, dispossessed of land and property, or otherwise alienated and injured.[249]

Had it not been for the more than three thousand allies, notably from among the Mohican and Natick tribes, the settlers might not have withstood the initial Amerindian assault. Had these native Americans joined Philip, he might well have exterminated the settlers. Yet most were rewarded by having their crops wasted, homes burned and possessions plundered. Many were relocated from their homes just before harvest time, leaving them to starve. At the suggestion of John Eliot, some were exiled to the barren (and by now misnamed) Deer Island in Boston Harbor. Relief supplies to these displaced persons was slow in coming and many perished of exposure and starvation. It was the general opinion of the period diarists that the praying Indians never returned to their former level of prosperity.[250]

After King Philip's War

By 1677 the General Court had consolidated the praying Indians into just four villages and they were not permitted to leave their own villages without express permission from the Court. In 1681 the number of towns was reduced to three. Those who remained in Massachusetts had be instructed in Christianity. They were strongly encouraged to wear their hair short in the manner of the English and abandon their scalp lock style. They were forbidden to carry firearms, required to obtain travel permits, and prohibited from entertaining strangers in their homes. Rebellious and rogue Amerindians could be

---

[249] Schultz, Eric B.; and Michael J. Tougias. *King Philip's War: The History and Legacy of America's Forgotten Conflict.* W.W. Norton, 2000; Richard Slotkin; and James K. Folsom. *So Dreadful a Judgement: Puritan Responses to King Philip's War.* Middletown, CT: Weysleyan University Press, 1978.

[250] Lepore, Jill. *The Name of War: King Philip's War and the Origins of American Identity.* New York: Vintage Books, 1999; Daniel R. Mandell. *King Philip's War: Colonial Expansion, Native Resistance, and the End of Indian Sovereignty.* Johns Hopkins University Press, 2010.

enslaved and sent to the West Indies or imprisoned.[251]

On 2 June 1685, the General Court of New Plymouth enacted a comprehensive militia law. The law required militia service of all able-bodied freemen and indentured servants and mandated attendance at periodic military training sessions. Exempted were physicians, magistrates, ministers, school masters, the colony's secretary, clerks of courts, sheriffs, constables, herdsmen, millers, masters of ships, seamen, and heads of households who had three or more sons enlisted in the militia. Physicians could write letters of exemption for those who were physically unable to serve, whether on a permanent or temporary basis.[252] The royal charter of 17 October 1691 formally incorporated Plymouth and Maine within Massachusetts, ending the necessity for a separate body of laws for these colonies.

In 1680, Massachusetts Governor Simon Bradstreet wrote to the London Company concerning the militia. The militia was not selective, but it enlisted all men except "Negroes and slaves whom wee arme not."[253] In 1693 the General Court again affirmed that all blacks and Amerindians were to be "exempted from all trainings."[254] An Act for regulating the militia was adopted on 22 November 1693.

> Whereas, for the honor and service of their majesties, and for the security of this their province against any violence of invasion whatsoever, it is necessary that due care be taken that the inhabitants thereof be armed, trained and in a suitable posture and readiness for the ends aforesaid, and that every person may know his duty and be obliged to perform the same, Be it therefore enacted by His Excellency the Governor, Council and Representatives in General Court Assembled, and it is ordained and enacted by the authority of the same. . .

---

251 *Mass. Col. Rec.* 5: 136, 327; *Proceedings of the Massachusetts Natural Historical Society and Library Association*, 1; Senate Document 95, 48th Congress, 2d Session, 46-47. See also George E. Ellis. *The Red Man and the White Man.* Boston, 1882, 459-63; J. Goodkin, "An Historical Account of the Doings and Sufferings of the Christian Indians in New England in the Years 1675, 1676, and 1677, diary in possession of American Antiquarian Society; Senate Executive Document 95, 48th Congress, 2d Session, 45-47.

252 *General Laws of the Inhabitants of the Jurisdiction of New Plimouth.* Plymouth: General Courts, 1685, 51.

253 Simon Bradstreet to Privy Council, 18 May 1680, in James Savage, editor, "Gleanings from New England History," *Collections of the Massachusetts Historical Society*, third series, 7 (1843), p. 336.

254 *Acts and Laws of the General Court of Massachusetts, 1692-1719.* London, 1724, p. 51.

Sec. 1. That all male Persons from sixteen years of age to sixty . . . shall bear arms and duely attend all musters and military exercises of the respective troops and companies where they are enlisted or belong, allowing three month's time to every son next after coming to sixteen years of age, and every servant so long after his time is out, to provide themselves with arms and ammunition, &c. . . . Section 12. That the persons hereafter named be exempted from all trainings, viz., . . . indians and negroes. . . . Section 26. That all persons exempted by this law from trainings shall, notwithstanding, be provided with arms and ammunition compleat, upon the same penalty as those that are obliged to train.[255]

In 1672 the militia of Massachusetts numbered fifteen thousand men, although only six thousand of these men had the right to vote or to hold political office.[256] More men could vote on their militia officers than could vote on their political officers. The patience and organization paid off. Jasper Danckaerts, who had severely criticized the New York militia in 1680, found the militia in Boston to be most impressive.[257] In 1678 the colony restricted shooting and arms practice near public or privately owned buildings for the protection of the citizenry.[258] In 1692 the General Assembly repeated the orders concerning the arming of the militia, but restricted the bearing of arms when the carriage might cause alarm or violate the general peace.[259]

Local militia companies were financed by militia fines. The company clerks collected the fines. They purchased the various supplies, such as firewood, gunpowder, match, flints, lead and food with these funds. On occasion they purchased arms and supplies for poor freemen.[260] The General Court imposed various duties and imposts to shore up the militia treasury at various times.[261] It also kept some expenses low by engaging in price fixing and by setting legal charges for services.[262] Still, supplies were often insufficient for the needs of the militia. For example, on 23 January 1694 Charles Frost reported to the General Court that, "for the great want of Shoes and Stockings

---

255 *Acts and Resolves of the Province of Massachusetts Bay*, 1: 128-30, 133.
256 *Calendar of Massachusetts State Papers, 1669-1674*, p. 332 [manuscript].
257 Danckaerts, Jasper. *Journal of Jasper Danckaerts: 1679-1680*. BiblioBazaar reprint,2008, pp. 239, 271.
258 Council of Boston, 28 March 1678.
259 *Colonial Laws of the Province of Massachusetts*, 1692-93. edited by W. H. Whitmore. Boston: State of Massachusetts, c. 1860, chapter 18, section 6.
260 *Mass. Col. Rec.* 2: 119.
261 *Mass. Col. Rec.* 1: 212; 2: 124; 5: 71, 76.
262 *Mass. Col. Rec.*, 5: 79, 137.

our soldiers here, several of them, are incapable of service for want thereof." Nathaniel Saltonstall agreed, reporting on the same date that his men were in great need of snowshoes for winter service and "ammunition, provisions and cloathing."[263]

During the winter of 1694-95 Lieutenant-governor Stoughton carried on involved correspondence with governor and council in Connecticut, trying to work out details of the defense of the region around Deerfield and along the Connecticut River. The principal issue discussed was how, when and under what conditions the militias of the two colonies could cooperate in the defense of an area of common concern.[264] In 1696 the General Court named one commissioner and authorized the governor to name a second commissioner to carry out negotiations with Connecticut and Rhode Island to defend the same frontier areas.[265]

In 1695-96 the home government requested that Massachusetts send troops to assist in the defense of New York. The legislature demurred and Governor Stoughton was delighted to hide behind it, writing that the requested aid could not be provided conveniently. For his part, Stoughton was delighted to have a scapegoat when pressured by the British authorities.[266]

The French attack on Haverhill, Massachusetts, was a major military engagement which occurred on 15 March 1697 during King William's War. Louis de Buade de Frontenac, Governor General of New France, dispatched French, Algonquin, and Abenaki warriors to descend on Haverhill, at the time a small frontier community. In the surprise attack, the Abenaki killed twenty-seven colonists, took thirteen more captive, and burned six homes.

The last battle of the war was on 9 September, known as the Battle of Damariscotta, in which Captain John March and his militiamen killed twenty-five Amerindians. Even after the war was officially ended, Abenaki raids on the English colonists continued. On 4 March 1698, Abenaki Chief, Escumbuit led a group of 30 Indians in a raid on Andover, Massachusetts, which raid was the last and most severe Indian raid on this town. There was also another raid by the warriors from Amerindians living in Acadia upon Hatfield, Massachusetts

---

263 *Collections of the Massachusetts Historical Society*, 43 [1909-10]: 512-14.
264 *Acts and Resolves, 1694-95*, c. 62.
265 *Acts and Resolves, 1696-97*, c. 76.
266 *Acts and Resolves, 1695-96*, cc. 29, 38.

in 1688, where they killed two settlers. In all cases, there was only the generally poorly trained militia available to respond.[267]

---

267 Grenier, John. *The First Way of War.* University of Cambridge Press. 2005, pp. 40-41.

The Massachusetts Militia in the Early Eighteenth Century

In 1702, perhaps in anticipation of full war, Queen Anne sent instructions to Governor Dudley. "All planters and Christian servants," she ordered, must "be well and fitly provided with arms." The entire militia was to be put in a state of absolute readiness and even indentured servants were to be fully armed against the expected invasion of the French and their Amerindian allies. All militia were to be mustered, trained and placed under adequate discipline. Still, the queen warned, "you are to take special care that neither the frequency nor the unreasonableness of remote marches, musters and trainings be an unnecessary impediment to the affairs of the inhabitants." Martial law was to be proclaimed only in case of extreme emergency and with the consent of council.[268]

The main tactics employed by Amerindians were offensive: surprise and destruction by deception. They preferred to attack in superior numbers and retreated when the odds went against them. They liked to surround an enemy and strike at dawn. One authority believes that they did not develop either tactics or strategy and were wholly predictable in behavior because they lacked the social structure to develop and execute advanced or complicated maneuvers; and they had not developed the imagination necessary to conceive of new methods of warfare. One of the greatest reasons for their downfall across North America was their inability to cooperate with other tribes, especially those who had been traditional enemies. Even their direction by European officers, English or French, did not change their way of fighting. Caucasian officers who were successful with the Amerindians in war found they had to follow the Amerindian practices rather than try to change them. The greatest influence that European officers exercised was in getting the Amerindians to make occasional raids during winter, as in 1704 on Deerfield.[269]

In 1704 the French and their Amerindian allies destroyed the town of Deerfield, on the Connecticut River in Massachusetts. The little town already had a history of tragedies. It was nearly annihilat-

---

268 Queen Anne's Instructions to Governor Dudley, 6 April 1702, in Kavanagh, *Colonial America*, 1: 318.
269 Turney-High, Harry H. *Primitive War: Its Practice and Concepts.* University of South Carolina Press, 1949, 125ff.

ed in 1676 during King Philip's War, and in 1694 a raiding party of French and Indians had barely been beaten off. As a result several of its forty-one houses were fortified, and a sentry had been posted nightly since war resumed.[270] On the last night of February 1704 a mixed party of two hundred French Canadians and one hundred and four Abenakis and Christianized Indians of Caughnawaga attacked, under the command of Captain Hertel de Rouville, veteran of the last war. The village contained two hundred and seventy settlers as well as twenty militiamen from neighboring towns, all apparently asleep. The surprise was complete, but the slaughter not as heavy as might have been expected.

Thirty-eight inhabitants were massacred and seventeen houses went up in flames, but at least half of the others found refuge in one or another of the fortified places. There was enough resistance for the Indians to lose eight warriors, and the Canadians three militiamen. One hundred and eleven prisoners were taken and sent north to French Canada at daybreak. The surviving villagers pursued the retreating raiders and inflicted thirty additional casualties on the enemy. For their part the Massachusetts militia lost nine men and failed to recover any captives.[271] Reinforcements continued to arrive in the Deerfield. By midnight, eighty militiamen from Northampton and Springfield had arrived, and men from Connecticut swelled the force to about two hundred and fifty able-bodied militia by the end of the next day. Following a debate concerning what action to take, they decided that the difficulties of pursuit were not worth the risks. Leaving a strong garrison in the village, most of the militia returned to their homes.

On the three hundred mile journey to Montreal, sixteen of the prisoners were killed, with several being burned at the stake, and two reportedly starved to death. The most famous captives were the family of the Reverend John Williams. The baby was killed at the outset, and Mrs. Williams was killed on the march, along with their Negro slave. Three sons, two daughters, and Rev. Williams survived the long trek. Eventually almost all the Deerfield survivors were ransomed and exchanged with Massachusetts. The notable exceptions

---

270 Calloway, Colin Gordon. *After King Philip's War: Presence and Persistence in Indian New England.* Hanover, NH: University Press of New England, 1997.
271 Haefeli, Evan; and Kevin Sweeney. *Captors and Captives: The 1704 French and Indian Raid on Deerfield.* University of Massachusetts Press, 2003.

were a few children, including Eunice, daughter of Rev. Williams. Even Governor Vaudreull could not obtain her release from the Indians. She remained with the Caughnawaga converts, converted to Roman Catholicism, married one of the Indians, and had two children. Thirty-six years later she was reunited with her brothers and sister for a visit, but the gulf was so great that she returned to Caughnawaga to live out the remainder of her eighty-nine years. Reverend Williams published an account of the massacre and capture which has remained the primary source of first-hand information on this event.[272]

Massachusetts raised five hunbdred and fifty militiamen to avenge the Deerfield Massacre. Command devolved on Colonel Benjamin Church (1639-1718), now sixty-five years of age and not in the best of health. Church decided not to pursue the Deerfield hostages, but to destroy the Abenakis by striking at the their towns and villages from Penobscot to Port Royal. Church's militia sailed out of Boston on 21 May 1704. Raiding along the way, they killed a few Amerindians and captured others, including the half-breed daughter of Baron de St. Castin, who had returned to France. The expedition burned Grand Pré on the Bay of Fundy and reached Port Royal, but at a council of war on July 14 Church and his fellow officers decided it was too strong to be taken with men, equipment and materials on hand. The force returned home with a hundred prisoners, mostly Abenakis, having lost only six men. Actually the militia had fought few, if any, real battles and achieved little except for the taking of prisoners and the burning and looting of the Amerindian towns. This was the fifth and last Indian expedition of Colonel Church.[273]

The governor and legislature set up a system of town-fortresses all along the two hundred and fifty mile-long border with Canada. Each town had its own militia. The linking and communication was provided by select militia which communicated on horseback, weather permitting, and on snowshoes during the winter. These strategic hamlets served as bases to launch attacks as well as defensive positions and havens for the population in times of trouble. This system,

---

272 Williams, John; Stephen West; and John Taylor. *The Redeemed Captive Returning to Zion: or, The Captivity and Deliverance of Rev. John Williams of Deerfield. New York*: Kraus, 1969 reprint of a 1908 edition of Williams's narrative.

273 Beattie, Daniel J. "The Adaptation of the British Army to Wilderness Warfare, 1755-1763," in Maarten Ultee. ed. *Adapting to Conditions: War and Society in the Eighteenth Century.* University of Alabama Press, 1986, pp. 56-83.

combined with strategic alliances with the League of the Iroquois and the general debility of the Amerindians allied to the French, served well to protect the colony.

As England prepared to enter Queen Anne's War (1702-1713) the monarch inquired of Governor Joseph Dudley, "how many [men] are fit to bear arms in the militia." It is unfortunate that his response cannot be located.[274] During this same time period Massachusetts used ranging units of minutemen, forts and regular militia, but it still cost the province about £1000 for each Amerindian killed.[275]

In 1707 the legislature decided that blacks living in the province were getting a free protection while whites had to serve in the militia. The legislature passed an "act for the regulating of free negroes." It read in part, "Whereas in the several towns and precincts within this province there are several free negroes and mulattos, able of body, and fit for labour, who are not charged with trainings, watches, and other services required of her Majesty's subjects, whereof they have share in the benefit." Section three provided that "all free male negroes or mulattos, of the age of sixteen years and upwards, able of body, in case of alarm, shall make their appearance at the parade of the military company of the precinct wherein they dwell, and attend such service as the first commission officer of such company shall direct, during the time the company continues in arms, on pain of forfeiting the sum of twenty shillings to the use of the company, or performing eight days labor as aforesaid, without reasonable excuse made and accepted for not attending."[276]

The legislature ordered that blacks be required to "do service equivalent to trainings." The legislature specifically mentioned substituting public service, such as highway maintenance for militia service. In times of crisis blacks were to report to the militia assembly to serve in whatever capacity they might be ordered. Failure to do public service was penalized by a fine of five shillings and failure to muster in times of emergency subjected a black man to public service of eight days.[277]

Legislative leaders of Massachusetts were highly irritated at

---

274 Queen Anne's Instructions to Governor Dudley, in Kavenagh, *Colonial America*, 1: 318.
275 Parkman, Francis. *Half Century of Conflict*, Little Brown, 1914, 1: 100.
276 *Acts and Resolves of the Province of Massachusetts Bay*, 1: 606-07
277 *Acts and Laws of Massachusetts, 1692-1719*. London, 1724, 1: 242.

New York by this time. The colony had refused to participate in the expedition and the British authorities had done little to encourage New York to participate. The cost in men and money had been borne exclusively by New England, and that meant, primarily by Massachusetts. What was much worse, Albany merchants were carrying on a quiet, but effective and profitable, trade with St. Lawrence River Indians. Moreover, plunder taken on Amerindian raids in Maine, New Hampshire, and Massachusetts turned up for resale in Albany shops.

A lull now developed, and it was French Governor Vaudreuil who opened negotiations for an exchange of prisoners in May, 1705. He controlled one hundred and seventeen New Englanders and he claimed to know of seventy more among his Amerindian allies. For its portion of the trade, Massachusetts sent to Quebec seventy prisoners, mostly Amerindians. The colonial authorities were greatly disappointed when they received only sixty Caucasians in return. Vaudreuil claimed that his Amerindians were independent allies, and, although he claimed to have used his best arguments and powers of persuasion, he had failed to convince them to yield their captives.

Legislators in Massachusetts now accused their own commissioner, Samuel Vetch, of prolonging the exchange business in order to carry on trade as a war profiteer among the enemy. Actually Vetch was carrying a secret letter to Vaudrenil from Governor Dudley proposing a truce of neutrality between the two provinces. Vaudreuil received it favorably but insisted on two conditions: that New York and the other northern English colonies be included, and that the English give up their fishing rights off Newfoundland. The first was difficult to comply with; and the second was impossible. Additionally, Vaudreuil continued to argue that he could not persuade his Amerindian allies to surrender their prisoners.[278]

Governor Dudley had sought help from England to capture Port Royal in Acadia and obtained nothing. English authorities clung stubbornly to the belief that the colonists could and should prosecute the war on or near their own soil. Colonel Church's failure against Canada focused even greater attention on the issue. Although some Boston merchants were trading illegally with the French and their Amerindian allies, most supported strong prosecution of the war in Canada. Boston fishermen were frequently driven away from fishing grounds off Newfoundland by French privateers operating out of Port

---

278 Haefeli and Sweeney, *Captors and Captives*, pp. 127-35.

Royal. Finally in 1707 Dudley asked the General Court to authorize and underwrite yet an enterprise against Port Royal. The legislature put out a call for two regiments, vessels were to be impressed, an English frigate in port was to be used and neighboring colonies were to be invited to join. The expedition sailed on May 13. New Hampshire contributed sixty men, and Rhode Island eighty. With the two Massachusetts regiments there was a grand total of 1,076 soldiers and about 450 sailors in the expedition.

The newly named militia commander, Colonel John March (1658--1712) was engaged in a variety of businesses in Newbury, Massachusetts. As a colonel in the Massachusetts Bay militia, he was active in a number of military operations against the French and Amerindians in both King William's War and Queen Anne's War. He was now facing a military problem quite different from his frontier service.[279] Massachusetts' Governor Joseph Dudley appointed Colonel March to lead the proposed expedition against Port-Royal, describing him as "a very good officer, & so well esteemed that I hope to impress no man into the service." The volunteer militia were landed in two parties and without much trouble drove the advanced French forces back into the fort, commanded by Governor Daniel d'Auger de Subercase (1651-1732).

March arranged the New England militia in a long semicircle and set up camp. Soon after, the militia disintegrated into a wrangling, unmanageable mob. There was a mutinous spirit among subordinate officers and the largely untrained and minimally disciplined militiamen. Add to that March's indecisiveness in command and the expedition was doomed to failure. None of the militia officers knew how to conduct a siege, and the soldiers, losing all confidence in them, reverted to behaving like the civilians which they actually were. The French forces at Port-Royal forces consisted of about two hundred men, strengthened somewhat by a small detachment of about sixty militiamen who arrived shortly after the siege began. Soon, additional help arrived in the form of some Abenaki warriors. Together the French and Amerindian forces put up a spirited defense. March retired to Casco where he was virtually relieved of his command by three commissioners sent by Governor Dudley.

After three councils of war about proceeding or giving up, the noble force decamped. Colonel March sent an apologetic message to

---

[279] "John March" in *Dictionary of Canadian Biography,* 2.

Governor Dudley, who, although deeply disappointed, demanded that March make another attempt at once. Dudley dispatched to Maine a hundred recruits, another frigate, and three members of the provincial council to advise March.[280] The expedition returned to Port Royal in August and found that the French also had been reinforced. For a week there was repeated skirmishing in the open, with several casualties, but no decision. On the second attempt to take Port-Royal in August, March's health and spirits gave way and he turned his command over to Colonel Wainwright Once more the New Englanders withdrew. Political leaders were vocal in its condemnation and demanded court-martial proceedings, but with officers accusing one another there were hardly enough left to serve as judges.[281]

Border raids resumed in 1708. The second raid on Haverhill was a military engagement that took place on 29 August 1708, during Queen Anne's War. Once again, as had happened in 1697, French, Algonquin, and Abenaki warriors descended on Haverhill. Governor Vaudreuil put together a force of one hundred Canadians and three hundred Christian Indians under Hertel de Rouville, of Deerfield fame. They were to be joined en route by eastern Indians and sweep the frontier once more. But the reinforcements did not appear, and many of the mission Indians turned back after experiencing what they considered to be evil omens. With his force reduced almost by half, De Rouville decided to strike at Haverhill, Massachusetts, on the north side of the Merrimac River. The village contained about thirty houses, perhaps one hundred and fifty people, and thirty militia in a picket fort. Just before dawn on 29 August the French and Indians struck. They met a spirited resistance as most of the inhabitants fired from their houses. The raiders tried to burn them out but were not successful. Stubborn fighting persisted for several hours. Relief troops came and tried to ambush the enemy, but killed only nine and wounded eighteen. After the attackers withdrew, the village counted up sixteen dead and three taken prisoner. The regional militia mustered and gave chase, and in a skirmish later in the day, nine of the French and Indian party were killed and some of their prisoners were

---

280 Kimball, Everett. *The Public Life of Joseph Dudley: A Study of the Colonial Policy of the Stuarts in New England, 1660–1715*. Longmans, Green, 1911, 121–23

281 Drake, Samuel A. *The Border Wars of New England, Commonly Called King William's and Queen Anne's Wars*. C. Scribner's Sons, 1897, pp. 72, 85, 129–30, 159–60, 227–28.

rescued.[282]

Haverhill was not the original target of the raiders. French authorities anticipated that their Canadian and regular French troops would be soon joined by a large number of native American warriors. Thus, the French commanders planned to engage in a series of raids on the communities of the Piscataqua River. However, some Amerindian warriors declined to participate in the expedition. That forced the French to reduce the scope of the operation and choose an easier target. The raid on Haverhill proved to be more costly to the French than previous frontier raids because the militia was now better trained and under more competent leadership.[283]

Late in 1706 Samuel Vetch (1668-1732) had embarked from England. A 38 year-old Scot, he was married to the daughter of Robert Livingston (1654-1728). Vetch was a newcomer to Massachusetts commerce, but he had seen enough of the war to become convinced that nothing effectively against Canada could be accomplished without military aid and leadership from home. The idea was prevalent in New York, of course, but Vetch had the energy and persuasiveness to present the glorious enterprise to influential government officials. There was something in it for himself as well. However, it took him two years to extract a favorable decision. He promised that 2500 colonial troops would co-operate, although his authority for making such a statement is surely suspect. Vetch thought it best if two battalions of regulars and six warships were dispatched from England with a regular military commander-in-chief to lead the attack on Quebec. Governor Dudley supported the idea, and so did Lord Lovelace, who was being sent to New York as governor to replace the corrupt Cornbury. The Board of Trade was slowly convinced by the end of 1708, and its recommendation was adopted by the ministry and the queen in February 1709. For his effort Vetch was given a colonel's commission to direct colonial preparations and was promised the governorship of Canada after it was taken. With Colonel Francis Nicholson, recently governor of Virginia, Vetch sailed for Boston.[284]

---

282 Drake, Samuel A. *The Border Wars of New England.* C. Scribner's Sons, 1897, pp. 240-47..

283 Haefeli, Evan; and Kevin Sweeney. *Captors and Captives: The 1704 French and Indian Raid on Deerfield. Un*iversity of Massachusetts Press, 2003, pp. 190-206.

284 Waller, George. *Samuel Vetch, Colonial Enterpriser.* University of North Car-

Fifteen hundred men from New York, New Jersey, Connecticut, and Pennsylvania, including the regular Independent Companies, were to rendezvous at Albany in May for an advance on Montreal. The Iroquois were to be brought into the campaign if at all possible. New England was to raise a thousand men to join with the English forces for an attack by sea on Quebec and Port Royal. Vetch was effective in arousing enthusiasm in all the northern colonies except Quaker Pennsylvania. Despite the sudden death of Governor Lovelace, New York moved with alacrity under Lieutenant Governor Ingoldsby and chose to participate actively in this campaign. John Schuyler was sent off to the Iroquois with gifts. Colonel Nicholson was accepted to command the forces gathering at Albany.

Never had the northern colonies co-operated so harmoniously and energetically, for they were all convinced that driving the French out of North America was the only means of achieving permanent peace. Although Pennsylvania had refused to furnish men, volunteers from the other colonies more than offset the defection. Everything was in readiness and anticipation high, but the British fleet and troops did not appear. In October Vetch learned that officials in London had quietly abandoned his scheme. Vetch cursed the day and returned an embittered man who had failed largely because he had not engaged in court politics and aristocratic intrigues. When the action at Port Royal did occur, the effort was chiefly the work of royal marines, and it was Port Royal, not Quebec, that would be the target. When Front Royal surrendered on 2 October 1710, American militia and volunteers had played at best a minuscule part. Vetch contented himself with a royal governorship at Port Royal, now renamed Annapolis Royal and his garrison troops were British regulars, not militia.[285]

In 1715 a militia unit under Captain John Lovewell (1691-1725) engaged a body of Amerindians in the Massachusetts territory of Maine. The Amerindians in Lovewell's militia broke ranks and pursued the attackers. This to an ambush in which the Amerindians killed many militiamen both from musket fire and in the hand to hand combat that followed. Lovewell's Fight, as the action was known, changed militia tactics somewhat, showing the great value of sustain-

---

olina Press, 1960.
285 Grenier, John. *The Far Reaches of Empire: War in Nova Scotia, 1710–1760*. Oklahoma University Press, 2008, pp. 17-18.

ing discipline.[286] In 1733 the legislature passed a act regarding the ownership of a militia gun.

> Act for Regulating the Militia. Every Soldier and other Householder shall always be supplied with a well fixed Firelock Musket of Musket or a Bastard Musket Bore, the Barrel not less than 3 foot and a half long, or other good Fire Arms to the satisfaction of the Commission Officers of the Company, a Cartouch Box, one pound of good Powder, 20 Bullets fit for his Gun and 12 Flynts, a good Sword or Cutlass, a Worm and Priming Wire, fit for his Gun, on Penalty of 6 Shillings.[287]

In 1721 the General Court enacted legislation which enabled the governor to impress or draft militiamen to serve with the British Army overseas as required to fill the assigned quota. He was allowed "to detach and impress, out of the militia; in the companies or troops under their command, so many able souldiers, furnished and provided as the law directs."[288]

In 1723, following the departure of Governor Shute, the legislature and the new governor, William Dummer (1677-1761), clashed with the legislature over control of the militia. Dummer accused the assembly of trying "draw off the forces" so the legislature assured Dummer that it merely meant to "draw off the pay and sustenance" of the military. Seeing that the power of the purse, as the house viewed it, meant, in reality, that the assembly would control the militia, Dummer answered that, while the legislature did have the power to appropriate money for all purposes, military included, he would not countenance any interference with his duties under the colonial charter to control the militia.[289]

The legislature was not through. It began to demand the submission of the journals and other records of field commanders that it authorized committee members to examine in detail and report to the whole body. The legislature had mandated that such journals be kept as early as Shute's administration, but it was not until it clashed with Dummer that it began its examination. Heretofore, the only reports required of militia commanders had been those routinely submitted in all colonies to the governor in his capacity as supreme military com-

---

286 Kidder, Frederick. *The Expeditions of Captain John Lovewell and His Encounters with the Indians.* Boston: Bartlett & Halliday, 1865.
287 *Boston News-Letter,* 7 February 1733.
288 Act of 23 August 1721 in *Acts and Resolves,* 2: 225, 333.
289 *Records of the General Court,* 11: 479.

mander.

The situation was impossible, of course. By involving the legislature so heavily in day to day operations, the legislature tended to undermine military discipline. If an officer was dissatisfied with his orders or assignment it appeared he could go over the governor's head and appeal to the assembly. Legislative tampering might suggest that advancement might come more rapidly by catering to the legislature than to the governor. If the officers and men had carried out a mission under gubernatorial orders, would the legislature withhold their pay or punish them? It had occasionally blocked pay and expense vouchers when it suspected financial irregularities, but it was nearly impossible to do so for policy reasons. Neither could the legislature withhold militia supplies and materials of war and thus weaken the colony in order to enforce its will on the governor and his militia. Even some responsible legislative leaders saw that by allowing politics to enter into military decisions and the deployment and discipline of the militia, the legislature had also invited insubordination. What it could, and did, do was to use its power of the purse to control the building, maintenance and garrisoning of forts, fortresses and fortified positions. It could also withhold appropriations and authorization for expeditions into other colonies.[290]

Cavalry units were not created or prepared for use against the native aborigine. The eastern and northern Indians did not begin to acquire large quantities of horses until about 1725 and by 1740 an Amerindian living in these areas who possessed no horse was a rarity. But even after acquiring horses, these tribes rarely used them to advantage in war.[291]

In early 1724 the legislature decided that it would issue pay and vouchers to militia units only after it had examined its journals and checked its muster rolls. It had come to the realization that it could not challenge the governor on policy matters, but it was determined to exercise as fully as possible what powers it did have. The reports that Shute and then Dummer sent regarding the legislature's interference with the military for a time put the colony's charter. Indeed, it was at this time that the English government issued the Ex-

---

[290] See Henry Russell Spencer. *Constitutional Conflict in Provincial Massachusetts*. Columbus, Ohio: Heer, 1905, pp. 121-25.
[291] Row, Frank G. *The Indian and the Horse*. University of Oklahoma Press, 1955, pp. 69, 222, 230.

planatory Charter, settling several problems in favor of the privy council. The home government thought Massachusetts had a surfeit of democracy and that its congress was attempting to usurp traditional and legal executive powers. It restrained itself from demanding a reduction in real legislative power, being quite satisfied that the legislature would return to its traditional and legal powers.[292]

By 1739 the freeholders of Boston had become concerned with their defense, holding that a defenseless town invited war.[293] The press in Pennsylvania, a colony that had no militia act of its own, reported with some considerable envy that Massachusetts had newly enacted its fundamental militia law. The new law required that

> Every inlisted soldier and other householder (except troopers) shall be always provided with a well-fixed flintlock musket, of musket or bastard musket bore; the barrell not less than three foot and a half long, or other good firearm, to the satisfaction of the Commissioned Officers of the Company; a knapsack; a cartouch box; one pound of good powder; 20 bullets fit for his gun; and 12 flints; a good sword or cutlass; a worm and priming wire fit for a gun. A penalty of six shilling for want of such arms as hereby required, and two shillings for each other defect , and the like sum for every four weeks he shall remain unprovided; the fine to be paid by parents for their sons under their command; for their servants, other than servants upon wages.[294]

When England declared war (War of Jenkins' Ear) on Spain on 19 October 1739, the American colonies were assigned quotas of volunteer militia to be recruited to assist the British regulars. The Massachusetts legislature offered a bounty for enlistments, but still had trouble filling even half of the quota which England had assigned to Governor Belcher. To increase popular participation, colonial militia volunteers were to be allowed to continue to elect their inferior officers. Officers and men would have rank and pay, and were to be armed and clothed, in measure equal to their professional British military counterparts. They were to "have their just share and proportion of all plunder or booty gained from the enemy, according to their services."[295] After the war they were to be permitted to retain their arms

---

292 Barry, Joseph. *History of Massachusetts.* 2 vols. Boston: Philips and Sampson, 1855, 2: 112-28.
293 *American Weekly Mercury*, 4 October 1739.
294 *Pennsylvania Gazette*, 11 October 1739.
295 *Boston News Letter*, 17 July 1740.

and uniforms for military duty.[296] Some five hundred volunteers from Massachusetts, along with volunteers from Rhode Islander, filled five ships when they left Boston harbor. After the British bloody defeat during the attack on Cartagena, West Indies, survivors barely filled one ship upon return. The colonists lost one hundred and fifty-three officers and thirty transport commanders along with untold numbers of enlisted men both to enemy fire and a fever which ran rampant through the encampment.[297] Approximately only ten percent of the volunteers had survived the expedition.

The militia Law of 1742 made parents responsible for the appearance of their sons and apprentices who were under the age of twenty-one at training days; also masters were held accountable for the appearance of their slaves and servants. Those responsible had to make certain their charges were present for various duties, such as watch, and also to attend alarms.[298]

On 25 October 1743 France signed a treaty known as the Second Family Compact with Spain and on 15 March 1744 joined Spain's war against England. The French made an unsuccessful assault on Annapolis Royal [Port Royal], Nova Scotia, in 1744. With a real threat to its security the legislature of Massachusetts took several steps to provide for the colony's defense. It increased military appropriations and increased militia training. And it appointed a new commander, Sir William Pepperrell (1696-1759).

Pepperrell was a prosperous merchant who spent much of his time in Boston and had served in the Massachusetts legislature and on the governor's council. Already a colonel in the Massachusetts militia, he recruited and commanded the New England volunteer militia which, in cooperation with the British Royal Navy, on 17 June 1745, captured Louisbourg, now in Nova Scotia. In 1746 Pepperrell was made a baronet, a title never bestowed heretofore to an American-born British subject. Because of this success, between 1754 and 1759, the British confirmed his command of all military forces of Massachusetts.[299]

In June 1745 Sir Peter Warren's fleet, along with Pepperrell's land forces, captured Fort Louisbourg while simultaneously Sir

---

296 *Boston News Letter*, 22 May, 5 and 26 June 1740.
297 *Boston News Leader*, 2 July and 6 August 1741.
298 *Acts and Resolves*, 3: 36.
299 Fairchild, Byron. *Messrs. William Pepperrell: Merchants at Piscataqua*. Cornell University Press, 1954.

William Johnson led his Iroquois warriors into Canada. The French retaliated by burning Saratoga in late November 1745. Massachusetts militia participated, primarily as volunteers, in the successful siege of Louisbourg, a French stronghold in Canada. Shirley was an early advocate of British destruction of all French forces in North America and the annexation of Canada. He was trained as a lawyer and emigrated to America in 1731 and held several posts in Massachusetts before serving as governor between 1741 and 1757. Following Braddock's defeat he was the nominal British military commander in North America. After he failed to capture Fort Niagara in 1755, his fate was sealed and he was replaced by Lord Loudoun The Board of Trade congratulated Governor William Shirley (1694-1771)[300] for his part in recruiting volunteers, equipping the troops and organizing the expedition.[301]

Immediately, the Massachusetts legislature began lobbying for the return of its provincial militia. While the militia was fighting at Louisbourg raids on the frontier had increased and the legislature wished to deploy the militiamen in defense of their own homes.[302] After the French incited Indian raids into Maine, all the New England colonies declared war on the Amerindian tribes allied with the French.[303] In late August 1745 the French allied tribes broke their treaty of neutrality with the Six Nations.[304] Shirley supported the legislature's demand for the return of the militia, informing the English that the militia volunteers were "to be discharged as soon as the expedition be over."[305] The militia was successful in repelling both French and Amerindian invasions thereafter, although calls for assistance continued to pour into Shirley's office until the end of the war. Some frontier towns demanded troops to garrison various forts and towns. Shirley agreed that hereafter no soldier would be sent out of the province for a period greater than one year, and additional militia would be enlisted, trained and equipped to replace any volunteer or impressed militiamen serving elsewhere.[306]

---
300 Schutz, J. A. *William Shirley, King's Governor of Massachusetts*. University of North Carolina, 1961. He served as governor of the Bahamas, 1761-1767.
301 *Boston News Leader*, 27 July 1745.
302 *Boston News Letter*, 1 August 1745.
303 *Boston News Letter*, 29 August 1745.
304 *Boston News Letter*, 5 September 1745.
305 *Boston News Letter*, 12 September 1745.
306 *Boston Gazette*, 22 April 1746; *Independent Advertiser*, 24 April 1746.

In April 1746 three British regiments relieved the volunteer colonial militiamen at Louisbourg. The British home war office conceived of another assault on Canada, with two armies leaving the colonies to attack the French. One army would move up the St. Lawrence River toward Quebec while the second would attack Montreal by way of Lake Champlain. Advertisements appeared in newspaper throughout the colonies, asking for enlistments of three, five, and seven years. As an incentive, Massachusetts offered volunteers £30 and a blanket and exemption from all impressment for two years following their return.[307] For its part, the British home government offered bounties in the form of land around Louisbourg to survivors of the expedition.[308]

The legislature argued that the militiamen would do better staying at home to defend against Amerindian raids. Governor Shirley disagreed. He argued that the tribes allied to the French had long been the greatest threat to the New England provinces and that the best way to end that threat was to carry the war into their villages. By striking at the heart of the problem the Amerindian threat would be destroyed for all times. This was properly an American cause and should be carried out by militia volunteers. The provincial forces on 30 April laid siege to the fortress at Louisbourg while the British ships blockaded the harbor. The provincial force suffered significant battle losses, while the British naval officers, who had a low opinion of American soldiers, grew increasingly critical of the American efforts. The great fortress at Louisbourg surrendered on 17 June. The provincials had lost one hundred and eighty men in combat, or to disease or at sea during the siege. At the same time, the Royal Navy ships did not fire on the fortress, and lost just one sailor. This produced friction between the provincials and the British. Adding to that problem, the terms of surrender guaranteed that there would be no plunder. However, the Royal Navy had captured several rich French prizes, and British sailors boasted of their good fortune.[309]

Although the British government had believed that the provincial troops were incapable of capturing Louisbourg on their own, the British demanded that forty-three hundred men be recruited from the

---

307 *Boston News Letter,* 5 June 1746
308 *Boston Evening Post,* 16 June 1746.
309 Carr, J. Revell. *Seeds of Discontent: The Deep Roots of the American Revolution 1650–1750.* Walker & Company, 2008, pp. 265-81..

colonies, but they themselves were unable to release any troops from home because all available men were fighting on the Continent. The home government expressed great surprise at their success, angering the Americans[310] The war ended with the Treaty of Aix-la-Chapelle signed on 18 October 1748.

The Louisbourg matter was not quite finished. A pamphlet appeared which was extensively reviewed, extracted, and debated in the New England newspapers. The anonymous author contended that there was no clear authorization from Britain to undertake the mission; that the authorities knew that the war was going to end and that Louisbourg would be returned to the French; and that the New England colonies had incurred enormous expenses which the mother country would not refund. Quite serious was the charge that the militia had been illegally and illicitly removed from the province, leaving its borders open for attack and leaving the inhabitants at the mercy of the marauders. The first obligation of the militia was the protection of the home folks, and not to act as a reservoir of trained manpower for military operations beyond the colonies' borders. Weakening of the colony's defenses to provide troops for service in any foreign land was unconscionable. Moreover, the impressment or recruitment of militiamen for dreary and unproductive foreign service had a deleterious effect on morale in the militia.[311] The same certainly could have been said of the recruitment of troops for the ill-fated West Indian campaign.

Simultaneously, Governor Shirley had been trying to finance a campaign to capture Fort St. Frédéric (Crown Point), which he considered to be an absolute necessity if the French were to be expelled. His sole method of financing this crusade was the issuance of more paper money. The other provinces failed to support the effort so the campaign was abandoned, but there was still the resulting inflation helped turn supporters of Shirley against him. The return of of Louisbourg to the French increased public dissatisfaction with Shirley, who was seen as complicit in British scheming against the colonies. Even William Pepperrell joined the large number of citizens calling for Shirley's removal.[312]

---

310 *Boston News Letter,* 2 July 1746.
311 *Boston News Letter,* 10 June 1748; *Independent Advertiser,* 27 June and 4 and 11 July 1748.
312 Carr, *Seeds of Discord,* pp. 308-13.

The Seven Years War

In the autumn of 1754 Governor Shirley wrote to the Earl of Halifax to report that he had experiences great difficulties during the previous summer raising 800 men to deal with the French who he was "certain had made a considerable progress in building forts" within Massachusetts. He also reported that the French had begun to establish permanent settlements within the province and that he was hard-pressed to recruit men to build and man the forts designed to protect the colony from further encroachments by the French.[313] In November 1754 the Board of Trade appointed Shirley to command two new American regiments and gave him the order to recruit, and draft if necessary, one thousand American colonials to serve. Moreover, the Board of Trade ordered that militia regiments be raised in Virginia, North Carolina, Maryland, and Pennsylvania and placed under the command of Sir Peter Halket and Colonel Dunbar.[314]

At the same time Shirley was forced to deal with a problem that also plagued Pennsylvania authorities: enlistment of indentured apprentices and servants. The province had recently had good luck with its efforts to recruit men, but "the great Dispute on this recruiting Service has been enlisted Servants. The [debate] has been carried on to a great Height in Pennsylvania and Maryland. I have always declared it was my opinion that His Majesty has an undoubted right to the voluntary services of His Subjects."[315]

In 1754 the Massachusetts General Court had enacted two laws dealing with offenses committed within the military, to be administered by courts-martial, and extended for an indefinite period of time. The Press Act dealt with the pilferage of arms, supplies and equipment. The Mutiny Acts applied to crimes which were uniquely military, such as mutiny, sedition and desertion, and conspiracy to commit these forbidden acts.[316] Although many had been passed previously, no mutiny act had ever been applied in time of peace, and all of them heretofore, carried a one year limitation [unless the enlistment

---

313 William Shirley to Halifax, 10 August 1754, in Stanley Pargellis.ed. *Military Affairs in North America, 1748-1765*. Hampden, Ct.: Anchor, 1969, pp. 25-26.

314 "Sketch of Regulations & Orders Proposed Relating to Affairs of North America," in Pargellis, *Military Affairs,* 24-35.

315 William Shirley to Halifax, 10 August 1754, supra.

316 *Acts and Resolves, Public and Private, of the Province of Massachusetts*. Boston: State of Massachusetts, 1908, 3: 737, 753-54.

ended earlier], and expired after 365 days unless re-enacted. Mutiny acts specifically refused to exempt men from the provisions of civilian due process. Courts-martial might recommend a death sentence, but it could not be imposed without the concurrence of the provincial governor acting in his capacity as commander in chief of the colony's military. Puritanical New England lawmakers concluded from their study of the Holy Bible that the good book limited corporal punishment to thirty-nine lashes. The law implied, if not specifically allowed, that militia units apply certain punishments including the lash within the noted limits. They also might impose the running of a gauntlet and riding the wooden horse and perhaps a few other relatively minor physical punishments. Greater penalties were reserved to the civilian courts and political authorities.[317]

Desertion had occasionally been a problem before imposition of the Mutiny Act, but these were usually handled by the officers. Colonel Richard Sykes related an incident that had happened in the earliest days of the Seven Years War. It concerned "a person that was willing to enlist under me and accordingly I enlisted him and paid him his Bounty, but he took the first opportunity to desert and I missed him instantly and advertised him and [offered a reward] of 20 shillings sterling for taking him before a magistrate."[318]

In light of the growing threat from French Canada, the colonial authorities decided to create a Committee of War and so designated five individuals to serve, including the governor, the deputy governor. Other members were chosen from among the town assistants, and the local militia colonel, lieutenant colonels, majors, and captains. The Committee effectively integrated the part-time militia into a full-time provincial experience. It agreed to require four training days per year for the train bands. While examining the state of military affairs, the Assembly learned there was only one fort and it mounted twenty-six small cannon. There were eight thousand two hundred and sixty-two men, able to bear arms and approximately fifteen hundred serving as privateers.[319] In February 1755, New York Governor William Shirley requested three thousand men to be raised to fill the provincial regiments.

---

317 Anderson, Fred. *People'S Army: Massachusetts Soldiers and Society in the Seven Years' War.* University of North Carolina Press, 1984, pp. 123-25.

318 Richard Sykes to Samuel Phillips Savage, 9 July 1759, in *Massachusetts Historical Society Collections*, 43: 653.

319 *R. I. Col. Rec.*, 6: 124-25.

In June 1754, the New England colonies all sent delegates to Albany to attend a meeting of commissioners to discuss the common defense of the colonies. Delegates purposed that they form a committee to create a "Plan of Union" to be submitted for the approval of Parliament and paid for at the expense of the colonies. As concerned the militia, the idea was to create overall administration under a president general and a grand council which would plan joint colonial military actions for the overall defense of the colonies. A wide array of opposing ideas, objectives, aims, and interests doomed the conference from the start.[320]

In 1734, the French had begun construction of a fort at a strategic location on the shore of Lake Champlain. Fort Saint-Frédéric was built at a narrow point in the lake, where its cannons could block any unwanted movement along the water. The route from Lake George, to Lake Champlain, to the Richelieu River was one of the few possible avenues for a British invasion of New France, and Fort Saint Frédéric was the colony's first line of defense in the region. This fort also served as a base for raids against the British colonial frontiers. In late 1755, at the beginning of the Seven Years War, the British targeted Fort Saint-Frédéric.[321]

In 1754, the French had made a bold and decisive move into western Pennsylvania, securing their advance with a fort at the junction of the Youghioheny and Monongahela Rivers, which join to create the Ohio River. The British, which had never buttressed their claims in the thirteen colonies with regular troops, dispatched a major army, backed by colonial militia, to remove the French. The home government appointed Major General Edward Braddock, the most senior general in the British Army, to expel the French from western Pennsylvania and the Ohio country.[322]

General Braddock conceived a multi-faceted assault on the French in North America. There would be an attack on Nova Scotia along with a three-pronged attack against the French. He would per-

---

[320] Shannon, Timothy J. *Indians and Colonists at the Crossroads of Empire: The Albany Congress*. Cornell University Press, 2000.

[321] Folwell, Elizabeth, and Amy Godine, *Adirondack Odysseys*. Blue Mountain Lake, New York: The Adirondack Museum, 1997.

[322] Hall, Richard, "The Causes of the French and Indian War and the Origins of the 'Braddock Plan': Rival Colonies and Their Claims to the Disputed Ohio," *Atlantic Politics, Military Strategy and the French and Indian War*: (2016), pp. 21–49.

sonally lead the assault through the wilderness of western Pennsylvania and siege Fort DuQuesne. The part of Braddock's scheme had failed miserably,m largely because of Braddock's total incompetence in conducting frontier warfare. Governor Shirley, now commissioned as a major general, and second-in-command of the British Army, had been assigned to assault the French fort near Niagara. William Johnson (1715-1774) was to was assigned to lead his Mohawk warriors, accompanied by a minimal number of colonial soldiers, to capture Fort St. Frédéric.[323]

In this engagement, the British troops suffered their worst defeat of the colonial period at the Battle of the Wilderness at Monongahela, near Pittsburgh, on 9 July 1755. Only bold action by Virginia and Maryland militia saved the remnants of the British Army from total annihilation. The survivors fled in terror to Cumberland, Maryland, and then on to the eastern seaboard. Braddock's defeat was a major setback for the British in the early stages of the war with France and was one of the most disastrous defeats for the British in the nation's history. General Edward Braddock (1695–1755), the most senior British commander, who led the British forces and was mortally wounded in the effort. Braddock had chosen to ignore all American advice, since he considered the colonials to be his inferiors.

The public was shocked. It could not believe that such a great army could be so soundly defeated by a numerically far inferior mixed force of native aborigine, militia, and a small number of regular troops. After Braddock's defeat most Americans became disenchanted with the European wars and the never ending struggle between two European rivals with its consequent repercussions for America. No longer did eager subalterns march into towns, line up and beat the drum and blow the trumpet and find dozens of able bodied militiamen ready to try a term of enlistment as volunteers in British regiments. American authorities discouraged the use of standard British impressment techniques.

A correspondent known solely as C.B. wrote in the *Boston Gazette*, comparing Braddock to tragic heroes of ancient times. He penned an ode to the *Questos de Ohio* [Seekers of Ohio] entirely in Latin. He invoked Virgil's *Aeneid*, which many regard as the classic

---

[323] Russell, Peter, "Redcoats in the Wilderness: British Officers and Irregular Warfare in Europe and America, 1740 to 1760," *William and Mary Quarterly*, 35: 4 (1978) pp. 629–652.

story of defeat and redemption. C.B. suggested that although Braddock's men were defeated they, like the Trojan Aeneas, would again be victorious. Thus, Braddock became an Old English Hero who was bravely slain in a righteous cause.[324]

Emboldened by the success of the French, whom the native aborigine saw as trading pardners, not as land-stealing settlers as were the British, Amerindian tribes in the northeast and middle colonies attacked British settlements, killing and burning as they went. Even several tribes which had little history of antagonism with colonists joined in. The frontier was indeed aflame.

Although Braddock was now dead, the home government decided to continue to execute the bold plan which had brought him to America. The campaigns against Nova Scotia and Crown Point were to be executed funded by the colonies and the ranks filled by colonials. Rhode Island supported the effort strongly and enthusiastically recruited men to serve and funds with which to pay its share. The British campaign against what was later known as Crown Point precipitated the Battle of Lake George which was fought on 8 September 1755, in the north of the New York. This was a most important part of the campaign by the British to expel the French from North America, following the British defeat at the Battle of the Wilderness. French General Jean-Armand, Baron de Dieskau (1701-1767), led a variety of regulars and irregulars. Many of Dieskau's troops were Canada-born French colonials and their Amerindian allies, not French regulars. The French sent approximately three thousand men, French Regulars, Canadians, to Crown Point. The "Lord of the Mohawks" Sir William Johnson led the British army which consisted solely of fifteen hundred colonial militia and two hundred Iroquois warriors. In early August an advance party under the command of Major General Phineas Lyman established Fort Lyman, which was later renamed Fort Edward, at the head of Lake George. Johnson led the Provincial forces, along with its artillery, and stores northwest from Albany.[325]

Sir William Johnson received intelligence that the French, with approximately six thousand fighting men, were in transit, intending to fortify Fort St. Frédéric and to establish a fort at the passage between

---

324 *Boston Gazette,* 11 August 1755.
325 Griffith, William R. *The Battle of Lake George: England's First Triumph in the French and Indian War.* Charleston, SC: The History Press, 2016; Harrison, Bird. *Navies in the Mountains: The Battles on the Waters of Lake Champlain and Lake George, 1609–1814.* Oxford University Press, 1962.

Lake St. Sacrament and Lake Champlain.[326] Johnson's Mohawk scouts had reported the French to be near Fort Edward. Johnson dispatched a thousand provincials under the command of Colonel Ephraim Williams, along with two hundred Mohawk warriors under the command of Chief Hendrick, to intercept the force. On the morning of 8 September at approximately nine o'clock, Williams, Hendrick, and their force departed from Fort Edward along the portage road where Dieskau's men were positioned. Williams commanded the militiamen from Massachusetts and Connecticut.[327]

A deserter warned the French of the impending attack. The French grenadiers blocked the portage road while the Canadian militia and their Amerindian allies prepared to ambush the British from both sides of the road just south of the present-day Lake George. Williams, neglected to deploy flanking parties or scouts. The colonial militia marched into the trap. Williams and several other officers were killed as were a substantial number of the militiamen. More still would have been killed had not some of the French-allied Seneca fired their muskets in the air as a warning to their Mohawk brethren in the colonial lines. Still, Mohawk Chief Hendrick and at least thirty of his warriors were killed in the initial volley of fire. Rearguard action saved the rest of the Amerindians and colonials.[328]

Hearing the sounds of battle, Johnson sent a relief column under the command of Lieutenant Colonel Cole with three hundred Rhode Island provincials. Cole and the Rhode Island militiamen arrived in time to effect the rescue of what remained of Williams' command. These men, along with reformed parts of William's force, were able to blunt the French assault, giving Johnson time to strengthen the defenses of the camp.[329] One cannot help but contrast this action with the extreme rigidity displayed by Braddock in his ignominious defeat. The New England militia took individual action to avoid slaughter while Braddock required his troops to retain strict and inflexible mili-

---

326 This fortification the English called Ticonderoga and the French named it Fort Carillon. Anderson, *Crucible of War,* p. 118
327 Anderson, Fred. *Crucible of War: The Seven Years War and the Fate of Empire in British North America, 1754–1766.* Faber and Faber, 2000 118.
328 Much of what is assumed to be true of this engagement is taken from a publication by the Society of Colonial Wars in the State of New York, *Account of the Battle of Lake George: September 8th, 1755.* New York, April 1897.
329 Ibid.

tary posture, leading to virtual annihilation.[330]

For his part, Dieskau chose to follow up with a direct attack on Johnson's camp. Among the first French casualties was Jacques Legardeur de Saint-Pierre, commander of the Canadian and Amerindian forces. Disheartened by this loss, the Abanakis refused to fight, so Dieskau personally led a frontal assault with his French grenadiers. Dieskau was severely wounded and the attack failed with heavy losses. Having contained the French attack, the provincial militia, along with their Amerindian allies, counter attacked. Members of the provincial force leaped over the breastwork, pursing the French attackers, and capturing prisoners.[331]

Colonel Joseph Blanchard, commander of Fort Edward, had better luck. Seeing smoke rising from the first engagement, he moved forward, first dispersing the French baggage train, and then engaging the retreating French grenadiers. His militiamen inflicted heavy casualties on these French regulars and also captured many. They threw the bodies of the dead Canada-born French colonials, French grenadiers, and their Native American allies into the pool, later called Bloody Pond.[332]

As it was, Johnson's troops failed to capture Fort St. Frédéric Still, the British asserted that the strategic result at the Battle of Lake George was significant. Johnson had been able to advance a considerable distance down the lake. After careful consideration, and for a variety of reasons, some better than others, Johnson and his officers concluded that an attack on Crown Point would not be possible He consolidated his gains by building Fort William Henry in order to protect his gains. Johnson garrisoned seventy-two Rhode Islander militiamen at the new fort and disbanded the remaining provincial expedition force.[333]

In the aftermath of the battle, Cole was outraged that the newspaper accounts, especially in the *Connecticut Gazette* and the *New York Gazette*, made mention only of Massachusetts and Connecticut militiamen, totally ignoring the contributions of the other colonies in rescuing

---

330 Anderson, *Crucible of War*, p. 119.
331 Anderson, *Crucible of War*, pp. 118-22.
332 Reid, W. Max. "Sir William Johnson at the Battle of Lake George," in *The Story of Old Fort Johnson*. Knickerbocker Press, 1906.
333 Griffith, William R. *The Battle of Lake George: England's First Triumph in the French and Indian War.* Charleston, SC: The History Press, 2016. The French refer to this as the Battle of Lake Saint Sacrament .

the remnants of Williams' command, but in their vital role in repelling the French attack on Johnson's camp. As was common, the militiamen acquitted themselves well in combat in the frontier.[334]

Cole then promulgated his own version of the battle which differed considerably from the initial reports. Principally, Cole disparaged the role of the Connecticut militiamen and suggested that its commander Phineas Lyman had hidden, and not exercised command, during the battle as he had claimed. Cole also reported that, despite Johnson's having been wounded, it was William Johnson who had returned to exercise overall command, rather than Lyman having commanded as Lyman had claimed.[335]

In the wake if the abject failures in implementing Braddock's overall strategy, authorities in London made bold changes in the command structure. John Campbell, the fourth Earl of Loudoun, replaced Shirley as the Commander of North American Forces. They also dispatched Major General James Abercromby as Loudoun's second-in-command. Because of his extremely close association with the Six Nations, there was never any thought given to replacement of William Johnson. Indeed, London promoted him to be the Indian superintendent of the Northern Colonies.

In February 1756, there was a new plan which would involve nine hundred and fifty militiamen, supported by two hundred British regulars, who were to mount an assault upon the French fortress at Ticonderoga. Once that was successful, the troops would proceed to attack Crown Point. The force was to assemble at Albany the first week in February.[336]

As with Edward Braddock, one cannot question the skill, knowledge, ability, and leadership of either Abercromby or Loudoun in European style warfare, but this was not Europe and battles were fought quite differently in the wilderness. The French had long understood that and consequently won important engagements, such at Brad-

---

334 York, A. L. "The Myth of the Citizen-Soldier: Rhode Island Provincial Soldiers in the French and Indian War," Master thesis, U.S. Army Command and General Staff College, 2016, pp. 79-82. York based his analysis upon Milton W. Hamilton. "Battle Report: General William Johnson's Letter to the Governors, Lake George, September 9-10, 1755." Worcester: Published by the Society, 1964, which was reprinted from the *Proceedings* of the American Antiquarian Society, v. 74, pt. 1 (April 1964).
335 Ibid.
336 *R. I. Col. Rec.,* 5: 480, 483.

dock's Defeat. Even the most aristocratic Frenchman understood that he must never allow French-Canadians or Amerindian allies to think they looked down upon them as inferiors. British aristocrats continued to show class distinctions with colonials and to regard the Amerindians as stone age aborigine. Disregarding the minimally disciplined and ordered colonial militiamen, Loudoun was pleased to confine them to garrison duty. No aristocratic English officers would consider allowing the riff-raft serving under them to exercise the freedom and enjoy the rights which colonials demanded. Loudoun especially could not understand that his overbearing treatment of the colonials would cause them to desert and his army to disintegrate, yet in 1756 desertion rate hovered around ten percent.[337]

In March 1756 the French launched an unusual winter attack on Fort Bull on Wood Creek. Fort Bull was a key depot which su0pplied Forts Ontario and Oswego. In the French forces successful attacked Fort Bull and destroyed substantial supplies of provisions which had been destined to go to the Oswego garrison. That relatively minor battle effectively ruined Shirley's plan to attempt the expedition against Fort Niagara in 1756.[338]

In early August 1756, French General Montcalm, arrived with three thousand men in a force which included three regiments of regulars and several Canadian militia companies, along with their Amerindian allies. The French first captured nearby Fort Ontario, and moved on to assault Fort Oswego.

In 1727 New York governor William Burnet had ordered the construction of Fort Oswego, which by 1722 had been a trading post in the Great Lakes region. A typical frontier log palisade fort, Oswego established a British presence and was an impediment to French incursions from Canada. Loudoun entrusted Oswego's defense to a garrison of British soldiers. Forts Ontario and Oswego forts, guarded the waterway leading up the Mohawk River and crossing over to the Oswego River watershed. Although Oswego was the stronger fortification, it came under fire from one hundred and twenty cannons taken from the abandoned Fort Ontario. More than one hundred British soldiers were killed, many of them by the Amerindians after the fort had been formally surrendered. The French took fifteen hundred British prisoners, and destroyed the fort. The French victory

---

337 York, *op. cit.*, p. 75; *R. I. Col. Rec.*, 5: 500.
338 Parkman, Francis. *Montcalm and Wolfe*. 2 vols. Little, Brown, 1897, 1: 387.

persuaded many of the Six Nations to join the winning side.[339]

While it is highly unlikely that the New England militia could have changed the outcome of the Battle of Oswego, at least they were spared the shame of its capitulation. That catastrophe also serve to force Loudoun to pay greater attention to the colonials. Adding to the difficulties, smallpox broke out, disabling many and killing some. With sickness, poor morale following the catastrophe at Oswego, failure of the colonies to send full contingents to Albany, with the winter coming on, Loudoun decided to do nothing for the remainder of this year so he dismissed the militiamen and disbanded the regiment.

As he prepared for the 1757 season, Loudoun decided to implement the Royal Proclamation of 1754 which specified that there was to be only one field officer in each colony who would respond to a specified British officer. Loudoun, apparently having assumed that by issuing various orders, and by placing General Daniel Webb in command of two regular regiments and five thousand five hundred provincial soldiers, all would work well. Loudoun sent the provincial forces to the forts of Lake George, along with British Army troops. Loudoun then sailed with British Regulars to besiege Louisbourg. Some believed that Loudoun could not have foreseen the disastrous defeat of Fort William Henry in August of 1757.

By the end of July, the French had successfully recruited nearly two thousand Amerindians who were assembled at Fort Carillon. They made a splendid and powerful addition to the army of six thousand French regulars, troops de la marine, and Canadian militiamen who had already assembled. t Montcalm was preparing to lead this vast horde against Fort William Henry.[340]

The siege of Fort William Henry occurred between the third and ninth of August 1757. The French ranks, filled primarily by some two thousand native aborigine, were led by Louis-Joseph de Montcalm, who moved against the British-held Fort William Henry which was located at the southern end of Lake George, between New York and French Canada. The fort, built following Sir William Johnson's defeat of the French at their Fort Saint-Frédéric, was poorly garrisoned by a force of British regulars led by Lieutenant Colonel George Monro, sup-

---

339 Parkman, *Montcalm and Wolfe*, 1: 334-423. See also Stephen E. Patterson, "1744–1763: Colonial Wars and Aboriginal Peoples," in Philip Buckner; and John Reid, eds. *The Atlantic Region to Confederation: A History*. University of Toronto Press, 1994, p.152.

340 Anderson, *Crucible of War,* p. 187

plemented by provincial militia. Webb refused to send reinforcements to the beleaguered Fort William Henry. Without reinforcements or resupply, it was inevitable that Munro would surrender the fort and the provincial breastworks located to the southeast. After several days of bombardment and increasing casualty rates, Monro surrendered to Montcalm.[341]

The terms of capitulation included the withdrawal of the British garrison to Fort Edward and the release of the militia to return to their homes. It also required that the French military protect the British from the Amerindians as they withdrew from the area. In one of the most notorious incidents of the colonial wars, the French allies allies violated the agreed terms of surrender and attacked the departing British column, killing and scalping both soldiers and civilians. The savages took as captives women, children, servants, and slaves, while slaughtering the sick and wounded. Early accounts of the events called it a massacre and implied that as many as 1,500 people were killed.[342] The the New England colonies responded to the Fort William Henry massacre. Calling out militia and seeking new volunteers, one estimate is that the region raised 4,239 New England militiamen.[343]

In 1757 the British hoped to raise in the colonies a substantial American force to join the British regulars in the war on the French in Canada. Massachusetts Bay and New Hampshire were jointly assigned quotas of 30,000 men of the 12,000 men respectively. Massachusetts had been assigned by far the largest single quota of any of the British colonies in North America. This was not a good time for the colony to be asked to carry such a large burden. Lieutenant-governor Spencer Phips had found it necessary to ask the Assembly to pay the volunteers who had returned from Albany, New York, in the summer of 1757, following the abandonment of that campaign by the British army. The Earl of Loudoun could not pay the Massachusetts militia and volunteers because he had barely enough money to pay his won regular army troops. The legislature refused to increase taxation, es-

---

341 Starbuck, David. *Massacre at Fort William Henry.* University Press of New England, 2002; and Ian K. Steele. *Betrayals: Fort William Henry & the 'Massacre'.* Oxford University Press, 1990. This is the principal action in James Fenimore Cooper's *The Last of the Mohicans.*
342 Dodge, Edward J. *Relief is Greatly Wanted: the Battle of Fort William Henry.* Bowie, MD: Heritage Books, 1998.
343 Anderson, *Crucible of War,* p. 201. York accepts this number without question.

pecially to pay for a lost campaign, so the province was forced to issue paper money to pay the troops.[344]

The Massachusetts provincial mutiny law was suspended in 1757 when Lord Loudoun placed the militia and provincial volunteers under the British Mutiny Act.[345] This law carried far more severe penalties that the provincial law had ever imagined. Under the British act the possibility of appeal of a sentence to civilian authorities was impossible.[346] This law had already created a draconian system, based upon inhuman and brutal discipline. Sentences imposed under it included the brutal whipping, and even execution, of some of the enlisted men. The provincial law had limited physical punishment to thirty-nine lashes, the traditional biblical number given to Jesus Christ before the crucifixion. Under the British law as many as a thousand lashes might be imposed. To many provincials, this really meant that the law sanctioned execution by whipping. Even army surgeons were more likely to revive a man who had become senseless than they were to intervene to restrict the imposition of sentences.

The British military system had long been based upon the creation and maintenance of an absolute dichotomy between men and officers. The implementation of this distinction began with an absolute refusal of officers to learn even the first names of their men. The officers were taught to regard the enlisted men as low-life types, devoid of a real human nature, morality and sentiment. Most officers believed that enlisted men were capable of reacting to, and were necessarily restrained only by, the harshest possible physical punishment. This practice stood in stark contrast to the New England tradition in which enlisted men and officers alike shared religious services, food and drink, and a faith in democratic practices.[347]

It is certainly possible that the imposition of martial law on Americans were among the true causes of the climate of opinion that led to the Revolution and the Declaration of Independence.

---

344 Gipson, Lawrence H. *The Great War for the Empire: The Years of Defeat, 1754–1757*. Knopf, 1946.

345 "Mutiny Act" in Comyns and Kyd, eds. *A Digest of the Laws of England*, 4th ed, (1793), 4: 381.

346 54 Geo 3 c 10. See also Mutiny Acts, 54 Geo. 3. c. 25, s 94; 55 Geo. 3. c. 108, s 98; and 57 Geo. 3. c. 12, s 99.

347 Anderson, Fred. *Crucible of War: The Seven Years' War and the Fate of Empire in British North America, 1754–1766*. Alfred A. Knopf, 2000, pp. 267–285.

Following the reversals of 1757 it was inevitable that there would be changes made in the English military and political command. William Pitt the Elder (1708-1778), 1st Earl of Chatham, emerged as a strong political leader and served as prime ministers from 1766 until 1768. Pitt conceived a different strategy to win, far removed from Braddock's plan. First, he appointed General James Abercrombie (1706-1781) to be overall commander, despite his inexperience in frontier warfare. Field Marshal John Ligonier (1680—1770), First Earl Ligonier, who served as Pitt's chief of staff, then selected four additional professional military men to assist Abercrombie: George Augustus, Viscount Howe, to be second in command; Jeffery Amherst (1717-1797); James Wolfe (1727-1759), and John Forbes (1707-1759).[348]

One of Pitt's most important decisions involved colonial officers. Pitt understood the heretofore unpleasant relationship between British officers and their provincial counterparts. Under the previous rules, British officers paid no attention to colonial militia commissions. Pitt wisely ordered that provincial officers who held the rank "as high as Colonel inclusive" would be regarded as equal to their British Regular counterparts.[349] The Crown provided arms, ammunition and tents while the colonial governments were responsible for funding clothing, recruiting, and pay. Under Loudoun, recruitment was difficult because both the citizens and the colonial legislatures disliked and distrusted him. His dismissal aided recruitment and funding.

By June 1758, Great Britain had dispatched several regiments to North America and tens of thousands of New Englanders had enrolled in the provincial militia. Abercrombie was to command the attack on Fort Ticonderoga with a force of approximately twenty five thousand men, including all of the New England militia. Rhode Island chose to raise one thousand militiamen to fill its obligation. Placing much of the responsibility for recruitment on officers, the Assembly stipulated that no officer could assume his commission unless his recruitment quota was filled. The Assembly offered a bounty of £100 for enlisting, along with the usual blanket plus a knapsack. The Assembly also made it a crime to discourage any person from enlisting with a fine of £50, or thirty days in jail. The Assembly had or-

---

348 Anderson, *Crucible of War*, pp. 215, 233-234.
349 *R. I. Col. Rec.*, 6: 113.

dered the militiamen to march no later than 25 March, with a planned arrival at Albany by 10 April. As it was, even by its best effort on 11 June 1758, Rhode Island was deficient one hundred and fifty men.[350]

The expedition against Fort Carillon at Ticonderoga would involve the largest army ever assembled in America and would march under the command of General James Abercrombie, commander-in-chief of the British forces in North America. The Battle of Carillon, also known as the Battle of Ticonderoga,was fought on 8 July 1758. A French army of about three thousand six hundred men under General Marquis de Montcalm soundly defeated the numerically superior force of British first-line troops under General James Abercrombie. That commander, in the worst tradition of Edward Braddock, chose launch a frontally assault against the entrenched French position, resulting in needless casualties.[351]

There was no substantial force of provincial militia experienced in frontier war fare to save Abercrombie's force as had been the case in Braddock's defeat. After the terrible failure of their heroic assaults against the French lines, the morale of Abercrombie's army was at the lowest possible ebb. It had retreated back to the site of Fort William Henry, with multiple casualties.[352]

Abercrombie's absolute incompetence was further demonstrated in the British retreat for here he demonstrated his inability to effect competent command. A competent commander would easily have encamped at the Lake George landing, taken stock of the situation, and then undertaken siege operations against the French. Abercrombie, to the surprise of more experience officers in his army, ordered a total retreat. Abercrombie's behavior did little to build respect or confidence in British officers among the provincial militiamen. It also confirmed their judgment first made after Braddock's defeat that the British had no idea how to conduct war beyond European battlefields.[353] Just as had the French at Monongahela, once again the com-

---

350 R. I. Col. Rec., 6: 129-31.
351 Chartrand, René. *Ticonderoga 1758: Montcalm's Victory Against All Odds*. Osprey, 2000. "The battle at Fort Carillon: 'what a day for France! What soldiers are ours!' Montcalm marvelled as he raised a great cross to celebrate a victory 'wrought by God.'
352 Nester, William. *The Epic Battles of the Ticonderoga, 1758*. State University of New York Press, 2008. The British general's name may be correctly Abercrombie or Abercromby.
353 Nester, *op. cit.*, p. 157.

mander refused to allow his men to be trapped inside a fort. Instead, both Frenchmen had led their m

A British army of fourteen thousand men under General Amherst would attempt to take the fortress of Louisbourg. Wolfe served as second in command at Louisbourg. This was largely a British Army operation, with support from enlisted provincials.

The selection of General Forbes was fortuitous, if not brilliant. While Forbes was gravely ill during most of the expedition which he nominally led against Fort DuQuesne, he relied heavily upon Colonel Henry Bouquet (1719-1765) and together they overcame difficulties caused by the sheer incompetence of officers such as Lieutenant-Colonel John St Clair, who had been charged with several construction projects. Forbes chose to take a more direct route against Fort DuQuesne than had Braddock, starting from Philadelphia, to Carlisle, Bedford, Ligonier and westward through the Allegheny Mountains. Forbes' most significant contribution was in building relationships with local Native Americans, who previously refused to co-operate with the British. The Maryland and Virginia politicians wished Forbes to use Braddock's road, initially carved from the wilderness by the Ohio Company, citing their contributions of money and large numbers of militiamen during the first ill-fated expedition, and threatening to offer less of both if ignored. Forbes made the correct decision to cut a new more northerly road and soon the french abandoned Fort DuQuesne. The militia of the middle colonies, and not New England, assisted the British regulars in this expedition.[354]

The Battle of Fort Frontenac, which took place between 26 and 28 August 1758, was a major operation consisting almost wholly of New England militia. Fort Frontenac was a French fort and trading post located at the eastern end of Lake Ontario where it drains into the St. Lawrence River. British Army Lieutenant Colonel John Bradstreet led a force consisting over more than three thousand men, of whom only about one hundred and fifty were British regulars while the vast majority were provincial militia. This army besieged the fort and its garrison of about one hundred and ten Frenchmen and French-

---

354 Cubbison, Douglas. *The British Defeat of the French in Pennsylvania, 1758: A Military History of the Forbes Campaign Against Fort DuQuesne.* McFarland, 2010. See also Louis M. Waddell and Bruce D. Bomberger. *The French and Indian War in Pennsylvania:Fortification and Struggle During the War for Empire.* Pennsylvania Historical and Museum Commission, 1996.

Canadians and effected their surrender two days.[355] The British also confiscated goods worth 800,000 French livres including a significant amount of supplies destined for French forts in the Ohio Country. They captured more than sixty cannons, some of them being the British cannons the French had captured at Fort Oswego. Overall, the British seized hundreds of barrels of provisions.[356]

. In September 1758, William Pitt replaced Abercromby with Jeffrey Amherst . Pitt's strategy now focused in sending Major General Wolfe to move from Louisbourg and capture Québec City. Simultaneously, Amherst was to attack Canada through Lake George and Lake Champlain. Pitt assigned the colonial legislatures the task of raising twenty thousand militiamen to assist.[357]

Amhert's force landed successfully and established headquarters where Abercrombie had established his command post previously. He immediately ordered his artillery to fire on the French fortifications. Louis M. Waddell and Bruce D. Bomberger. *The French and Indian War in Pennsylvania:Fortification and Struggle During the War for Empire.*   Pennsylvania Historical and Museum Commission, 1996.Amherst reported to Governor Hopkins that as preparing to siege Ticonderoga, the French blew up a portion of the fort and retreated to Isleaux-Noix.[358] Amherst reconstructed Ticonderoga which was only partially destroyed. By constructing a fort at Crown Point, and by building roads connecting Ticonderoga, Crown Point, Amherst was preparing for an attack on French Canada. Professor Anderson in his Crucible of War, reported that Amherst disliked Wolfe and hoped that Wolfe's attack on Québec would fail and he would attack, winning the glory of ending French rule in North America.[359]

In August 1759, faced with a vastly superior British army advancing up the Lake Champlain Valley, the French abandoned Fort Saint-Frédéric, destroying it. Three hundred and twelve Rhode Island militiamen were present at this action under the command of Colonel Bradstreet. The French then retreated further into Canada. The British

---

355 Chartrand, René. *Fort Frontenac 1758: Saving Face after Ticonderoga.* Osprey, 2001.
356 Tomlinson, Everett T. *A Soldier of the Wilderness. A Story of Abercrombie's Defeat and the Fall of Fort Frontenac in 1758.* Chicago: W. A. Wilde Co., 1905.
357 4 Anderson, *Crucible of War*, pp. 307-310; *R. I. Col. Rec.*, 6: 178-80.
358 *R. I. Col. Rec. 6*: 217.
359 Anderson, *Crucible of War, p.* 343.

began construction of a new fort, calling it Fort Crown Point. The facility which the British constructed was at least one-third larger than the French facility. Fort Crown Point ultimately covered three and a half square miles, and it was intended to be the new center of British military power in the region. In April 1773, Fort Crown Point was destroyed by a fire which originated in a barracks building and spread to a nearby powder magazine.[360]

Pitt devised his plan to final victory in the winter of 1759. He intended to use the regular and provincial forces to occupy Montréal, the most important seat of French power in Canada. To achieve that goal, Amherst undertook a three-pronged attack into Canada. He personally led twelve thousand men from Albany to Oswego and then down the St. Lawrence. He dispatched Brigadier General William Haviland with three thousand five hundred regular British troops, aided by the provincial militia, from Crown Point to march on Montréal. Third, Brigadier General James Murray would lead three thousand seven hundred and fifty men assembled from Louisbourg and Québec down the St. Lawrence by ship.[361]

Amherst had hoped that the provinces would keep their recruits under arms over the winter of 1759-1760, but that was not to be the case. There already had been significant desertions and the terms of enlistment required that the militiamen be released soon. Much to Amherst's disappointment the provincial militiamen were tardy in arriving. He noted that none had appeared by 8 May. This was the reasonable result of men not wishing to march to a place so far away, the shortage of funds and low premiums offered, shortage of equipment, and general lethargy developed as the war drug on. All the colonies were nearing exhaustion in terms of both manpower and finances.[362]

Montréal capitulated on 8 September 1760, effectively ending the Seven Years War as far as colonial troops were concerned. Many of the colonial militiamen, including those from Rhode Islander, declared themselves "demobilized" themselves and returned home, with or without British of provincial approval. Colonial legislatures, as well as the British high command, viewed this act as desertion. For their part, the militiamen who deserted and returned home did so because they saw neither benefit nor further need for lingering so far

---

360 *R. I. Col. Rec.*, 6: 166.
361 Anderson, *Crucible of War*, p. 388; Parkman, *Montcalm and Wolfe*, p. 377.
362 York, *op. cit.*, p. 109.

from their homes in Rhode Island.[363]

One historian, utilizing newspaper advertisements only, looked at desertions from the military between 1755 and 1762. In that way, he identified one thousand six hundred and ninety-four deserters, of whom nine hundred were provincials. He offered the discriminatory treatment meted out by British officers as a primary reason for desertion. He might also have added the disgust many colonials felt at the brutal punishment the British utilized against all enlisted men.[364]

During the French and Indian War, Massachusetts had enlisted many slaves. At least on militia company showed blacks on its rolls.[365] In 1763 Reverend Jeremy Belknap, an early opponent of slavery, noted that the number of slaves in Massachusetts had undergone a precipitous decline because so many had enlisted in the militia, or served as volunteers, and had won their freedom by serving in the recent war. Still others had won their freedom, or merely escaped, by enlisting in the army or navy.[366]

We may think of the militias of the southern colonies exclusively when we think of the containment of slaves, but northern militias also had a certain responsibility in that area as well. Josiah Quincy, Jr., described the slave patrols of Massachusetts, on which he served. Local committees, as in South Carolina, were wholly responsible for enforcement of slave laws. The committees consisted of three justices of the peace who were empowered to enlist militiamen as a *posse comitatus*, arrest slaves for virtually any reason and tray and punish a slave at the place of arrest. A convicted slave had no recourse to appeal or any other trial.[367]

The British army, always hungry for manpower, used the New England volunteer militia in the French and Indian War as a reservoir of trained manpower upon which to draw for recruits. British recruit-

---

363 *R. I. Col. Rec.*, 6: 260; York, *op. cit.*, p. 110.
364 Agostini, Thomas, "Deserted His Majesty's Service: Military Runaways, the British-American Press, and the Problem of Desertion during the Seven Years' War," *Journal of Social History,* 40: 4 (2007), p. 976.
365 *History of the Town of Higham, Massachusetts.* 3 vols. Higham: Higham Historical Society, 1893, 1: 265.
366 "Queries Respecting the Slavery and Emancipation of Negroes in Massachusetts, Proposed by the Honorable Judge Tucker of Virginia and Answered by the Reverend Doctor Belknap," *Collections of the Massachusetts Historical Society*, first series, (1795), 4: 199.
367 Quincy, Josiah, Jr., "The Journal of Josiah Quincy, Jr., 1773" *Proceedings of the Massachusetts Historical Society*, 49 [1915]: 446, 454-57.

ing officers often neglected to explain that enlistment was for life. Garrison troops were much more likely to be kept beyond their terms of enlistment and pressured into agreeing to serving in the regular army than those troops assigned to combat duty. The walls of a fortress kept the enemy out, but made the commander a dictator within, holding for him all those who entered its ramparts.[368]

The governor of Massachusetts, Thomas Pownall (1722-1805), wrote to William Pitt in England, arguing against the deceitful and damaging practice of recruiting his citizens into the regular army. He used language that he knew would appeal to an English gentlemen, arguing that recruitment had been among the sons of the best people of New England, when, in fact, he knew that to his own people these class distinctions meant little or nothing. Pownall knew that the people of Massachusetts were far too democratic in spirit to care whether those impressed or enlistedwere themselves, or were the sons of, farmers, tradesmen, merchants or gentlemen.

> I beg leave, sir, to inform you that most of these soldiers in the ranks are freeholders, who pay taxes; that these are the sons of some of our representatives, the sons of some of our militia colonels, and the sons of many of our field officers, and other officers now doing duty as privates in the number I have this year raised. And that the sons of some of our principal merchants, who pays £500 sterling per annum taxes, were impressed for the same.[369]

Pownall believed that military service was to be undertaken only when there was a threat and the freemen could not long remain free if they allowed themselves to be enlisted into a system where even the most rudimentary freedoms were lost. After a war Americans believed that the military should be disbanded, or at least reduced substantially, and volunteers and militia should return to their homes and to normalcy. By reducing the military presence and dismissing most of the men, England would be guaranteed an effective fighting force should it be needed again. By continuing to bind a free people to an archaic, draconian and authoritarian military system, England risked alienating those on whom it had depended in the past, on whom it must depend in the future for defense in North America.[370]

---

368 Anderson, *People's Army*, 65-66.
369 Thomas Pownall to William Pitt, dated 10 September 1758, in *Parkman Papers*, 42: 285.
370 Anderson, *People's Army*, 61-62.

Massachusetts Militia in the Revolution

By early 1775, the Massachusetts militia had undergone some significantly changes. There were no longer the threats from the French and their Amerindian allies which had marked the previous decades. Consequently, the militia had lapsed as a military organization, and had taken on various non-military functions. However, beginning in mid-1774, there was renewed emphasis placed upon the militia's original purpose-the defense of the citizenry, causing the militia to assume a renewed importance. After 1774 it become militarily more effective and the colonists sought to recreate the militia with patriotic attitudes. Prior to its reorganization in 1774 it is unlikely that the militia would have acted as a unified body because of the several political divisions. The importance of the militia, however, cannot be assessed solely in military terms. The militia reflected many of the issues and conflicts that were crucial in pre-Revolutionary colonial society. Through both its leadership and the increased importance placed upon its role in the colony, the militia was directly involved in the crises as the Revolution approached. The militia became the focus of the conflict which witnessed a growing polarization and struggle for control. By 1774 the polarization had reached a point in which the differences between the opposing factions were virtually irreconcilable.[371]

The American, and especially the New England, colonists had endured many infringements of their liberty by 1775. As early as the 1760s the anonymous authors of the *Journal of the Times*, presumed to have been written in Boston, boasted that there were "30,000 men between Boston and New York ready to take up arms" in order to "throw off the dependance" upon Great Britain unless the mother country improved relations.[372] They disliked many of the English remedial remedies taken to insure continued hegemony over the colonies. The English had interrupted shipping and required that the colonies trade only with the Mother Nation or her other colonies. The Quebec Act, extending full religious toleration to the French-Canadians who were Roman Catholics, did not set well with the prejudiced colonial Protestants. They did not like the Quartering Act which al-

---

371 Boucher, Ronald L., "The Colonial Militia As a Social Institution: Salem, Massachusetts 1764-1775," *Military Affairs,* 37: 4 (1973), pp. 125-130.

372 *Boston Evening Post*, 3 April 1769.

lowed for the billeting of the King's soldiers in any home or ship. The Port Act had thrown hundreds of seamen and longshoremen out of employment. General Gage's troops cut off the city's provisions by sea, but they arrived by land in a wide variety of carts, wagons, and other conveyances.

Of the many acts Americans considered intolerable none was more odious than the Quartering Act. American intellectuals recalled Machiavelli's warning that standing armies in times of peace are most likely to get into mischief and to brawl with the civilian population. A New England minister in 1768 had noted that "wherever troops are quartered, the civil authority should have a strict eye over them."[373] *The Boston Evening Post* and other newspapers of the 1760s and 1770s frequently reported that soldiers quartered had committed various atrocities against the population.[374] One great objection to quartering of troops in peacetime was that it violated the English Bill of Rights and was thus viewed as an "intolerable grievance" to freemen.[375]

> One great objection to the quartering of troops in the body of a town is the danger the inhabitants will be in of having their morals debauched. The ear being accustomed to oaths and imprecations, will be the less shocked at the profanity and the frequent spectacles of drunkenness, exhibited in our streets, greatly countenances this shameful and ruinous vice. The officers of the army are not backward in resenting the smallest disrespect offered themselves by a soldier, and such offenses are severely punished, but it seems the name of God may be dishonored with horrid oaths and blasphemies. . . .[376]

Adding to the increasingly hostile atmosphere was the position and attitude of Governor Thomas Hutchinson (1711-1780). He seemed bent on promoting confrontation by advocating and enforcing policies that seemed to have been designed expressly to alienate the people of Massachusetts Bay. A fifth-generation descendant of religious protester Anne Hutchinson, Thomas was the son of a wealthy merchant who entered politics in 1737. He represented Massachusetts at the Albany Conference, having served as a delegate in the General

---

373 Quoted in *New York Journal*, 29 December 1768.
374 *New York Journal, Supplement*, 9 February, 6 April and 29 June 1769; *Boston Evening Post*, 1 May 1769.
375 *Boston Evening Post*, 1 May 1769.
376 Reprinted in *New York Journal, Supplement*, 12 January 1769.

Court and as judge. By 1756 he was considered the most able man in Governor William Shirley's administration. In 1758 he became lieutenant-governor and in 1760 chief justice of the superior court. He was a staunch conservative who opposed the growing sentiments for independence, such as opposition to the Writs of Assistance and the Stamp Act Congress.

When Governor Bernard returned to England in 1769, Hutchinson became acting governor, and, in 1771, governor. He defended the absolute sovereignty of the British parliament over the colonies. The fact that his family had long lived in the colony caused many to think him traitor to his own. Benjamin Franklin caused some thirteen politically incriminating letters to be made public. Despite this embarrassment, and the formal request of the General Court that he resign and leave the colony, he remained in power through the Boston Tea Party. The latter event was precipitated in some large measure because Hutchinson had insisted on collecting the hated tax on the East India Tea Company's popular product. Finally, Thomas Gage assumed office on 1 June 1774 and Hutchinson left for England, never to return to America. Governor Thomas Gage attempted to escape the unsettled, radical atmosphere of Boston by moving the General Court to Salem in 1774. However, Gage found the General Court that convened' in Salem as stubbornly resistant to his wishes as the one he had faced in Boston. By this time, the stage for open rebellion and insurrection was well set. Hutchinson's conservatism was well expressed after he settled in England in a rejoinder he wrote in response to the Declaration of Independence.[377]

Timothy Pickering was appointed Colonel of the First Essex Regiment two months later. Pickering instructed the local militia companies of Salem "to hold themselves in readiness to march at the shortest notice under the command of such officers as they shall choose."[378] It took only a minor crisis to prod Salem into serious military preparations.

Meanwhile, the French were enjoying the English discomfort. Their observers and political analysis knew that the Americans were well prepared and well armed and were spoiling for a confrontation.

---

377 Bailyn, Bernard. *The Ordeal of Thomas Hutchinson.* : Harvard University Press, 1974; Peter O. Hutchinson, comp. *The Diary and Letters of His Excellency Thomas Hutchinson..* 2 vols. Boston: A. M. S., 1963.

378 *Essex Gazette,* 13-20 December 1774.

They seemed to have been amused at the naivety of the English who were ignoring the obvious signs warning that trouble lay ahead. As early as 1774 the French newspapers observed that the militias of New England were prepared to repel force with force. The French press reported that Massachusetts Bay could muster 119,600 militiamen "all of good will and prepared to act if they must."

For its part the English press had little but disdain for their provincial cousins. The *London Publick Advertiser* of January 1775 had belittled the military prowess of the colonials. No American force could begin to think realistically of challenging the British force, the finest standing army in the world. Each disciplined British soldier was worth several of the backwoods militiamen. There was no true standing army, but if one should be formed each trained English soldier would be worth at least two of their opponents. The Advertiser's reporter declared, "The Americans, though in general of our stock, appear to me to have for the most part degenerated from the native valor as well as [the] robust make of the men in this country."

By the spring of 1775 the city was like a tinder pile, ready to be set ablaze by a single incident. Governor Gage had inherited a time-bomb from Governor Hutchinson and seemed to have no idea how to defuse it. The citizens had been fired up by earlier confrontations such as the Boston Massacre and the Boston Tea Party. The Sons of Liberty, the Committee of Correspondence and other patriotic propagandists were agitating among the population. The city had split its loyalties between the growing cause for independence and the United Empire Loyalists. Clashes between the growing the two native groups occurred daily. Patriots had good intelligence. Men like John Hancock, Francis Shaw and Paul Revere entertained the cream of the young and ambitious British officer corps, quietly, but efficiently, milking information on the number, arms, spirit and disposition of British troops.

In addition to serving as Governor of Massachusetts, Thomas Gage (c.1719-1787) was supreme commander of the King's forces in America. He had arrived initially in America to serve on Braddock's ill-fated expedition and afterwards fought successfully against the French. In 1760 he had been appointed governor at Montreal, and in 1763 became supreme commander at New York. His immediate charge in 1774 was to quiet agitation against various parts of the Intolerable Acts. He had been provided with four thousand troops in

Boston to keep the peace. He pondered his alternatives. Could he respond by using purely political means as governor or need he use the military force at his disposal as commander? Should he remain in Boston holding city, or should he move his troops into the countryside, pacifying the entire state? The decisions were difficult, but little might Gage have imagined how important these decisions would become.

Meanwhile, the Massachusetts colonial militia, long fallen into disuse and disorganization, was revitalized, disciplined, equipped and drilled. The colonial militia marched and the English marines and regular army troops counter-marched. Each observed the other with suspicion. While many senior British officers dismissed the rustic citizen-soldiers as suitable only to deal with the native aborigine, other officers saw a purpose in the militia training. If nothing else the gatherings patriotism. These factors proved to be far more important to the future of the nation than the actual military training and practice the meetings generated.

Many believe that the intellectual godfather of the revitalized Massachusetts militia was Timothy Pickering (1745-1829), an outspoken Whig. Pickering contended in his first letter written as "A Military Citizen," and published in the *Essex Gazette,* that a well-organized militia rendered permanent professional armies unnecessary on American soil." Thus it was extremely important that the militia be kept alive, well, and fully trained and equipped as it was the bulwark of the free people of Massachusetts. He asserted that the social structure of the militia should conform more closely to the hierarchical social order prevailing in colonial society in order to achieve the best possible militia. In 1775 Pickering had published *An Easy Plan of Discipline for a Militia.* Based upon a clearly pragmatic approach. Noting the limited time which was ordinarily available for training, he sought to simplify earlier manuals even more by eliminating "the custom and prejudice (that) are the foundations of many practices among the military, and maxims . . . blindly adopted without any examination of the principles upon which they are founded." The ordinary militiaman must understand the exercises performed, and if the motions are taught because they are "convenient, useful and necessary," they will be accepted and learned more easily.[379]

---

379 Pickering, Timothy as "A Military Citizen" in Octavius Pickering. *The Life of Timothy Pickering.* 2 vols. Boston, 1867, 1: 16. See also Timothy Pickering. *An*

The British officials had good intelligence.[380] There were more than enough Tory spies and other Loyalists to keep Gage and his staff informed of the events transpiring in the country. The British could observe the development of things in Boston first hand. When the British did nothing to prevent the citizen-soldiers from organizing these trained bands became ever more bold. Their governing body, the Provincial Congress of Massachusetts, met in Cambridge without British consent or legal authority. The Congress empowered the Committee of Safety, headed by John Hancock, to call out the entire state militia if the events of the day required. Hancock divided the militia into the regular citizen-soldiers and the select group, the Minutemen, who were to respond to any emergency at a moment's notice. Both militia groups were clearly extra-legal. There was no threat from foreign enemy or Amerindians. The reconstituted militia was wholly designed to counter English power.[381]

None of this had been lost on Gage or on most of his officers. He opted to use some military measures against the colonists. Gage knew what military measures were being taken in both the city and the surrounding countryside. Some of the militia appropriated some of the colony's artillery. The Congress voted to equip a militia of no less than fifteen thousand men. A powder magazine and armory were set up in Concord.[382] Legislation had long required that each man retain a certain measure of gunpowder and lead for bullets. One pound

---

Easy Plan of Discipline of a Militia. Salem, MA, 1775, pp. 3-4, 11-12

380 See Franklin B. Hough. *General Gage's Informers.* University of Michigan Press, 1932.

381 The account of the events at Lexington and Concord given here largely follows *The American Heritage Book of the Revolution.* American Heritage, 1958, pp. 46-119; and John R. Alden, *A History of the American Revolution.* Knopf, 1969, pp. 173-78.

382 A large quantity of provisions and military stores being deposited here, induced General Gage, who commanded the British troops at Boston, on the memorable 19th of April 1775, to send a detachment to destroy them. Who, after they had thrown a considerable quantity of flour and ammunition into the mill pond, knocked off the trunnions and burnt the carriages of several field pieces, and committed other outrages, were opposed at the North bridge by the militia of this and several other towns . . . . While the troops were in town, they fired the court house, in the garret of which there was a great quantity of powder. This fire, by the intercession of one Mrs. Moulton, a woman of above 80 years of age, the troops extinguished; otherwise the houses adjoining, would have been destroyed. . . . These depositions are recorded in the town books of Concord . . . . [*Massachusetts Historical Society Collections*, 1: 240-41].

of powder might have been sufficient for a dozen shots. Individual powder-horns, fabricated from hollowed-out cow's horns, would rarely retain a pound of gunpowder, making a central supply absolutely necessary. Add to that the larger demands of even small cannon and a central powder magazine was indispensable.

The Congress appointed five generals -- Artemas Ward, Seth Pomeroy, John Thomas, William Heath and Jedediah Preble -- to head the trained bands. Gage decided that things had gone too far. The rebels must be disarmed. There was no end to their potential for military power.

The English colonial authorities considered taking away the colonials' arms, but rejected this idea because it was impossible to do. On 15 December 1774 Gage wrote to the Earl of Dartmouth, "Your Lordship's idea of disarming certain Provincials would doubtless be consistent with Providence and Safety; but it neither is, or has been, practicable without having recourse to force and being Master of the Colony."[383] In London, William Pitt, Earl of Chatham, on 20 February 1775, had moved that the House of Lords address the king, asking that the problems be resolved and a way found to establish the peace. Pitt asked that the "fatal acts of the last session be repealed." On 1 February 1775 he had moved a provisional act for settling the disputes in America, but the bill was rejected.[384] Conflict seemed to be inevitable.

In February 1775 Colonel Thomas Leslie led has 64th North Staffordshire regiment to seize the militia supplies. Apparently, Leslie had no thought of provoking armed conflict. When the militia of the greater Salem are mustered and confronted the British troops, Leslie withdrew and the militia supplies remained in colonial hands. The Minutemen had achieved their purpose. All knew that this was the first, unfinished chapter. A more active commander or more aggressive troops or an accident might make the next encounter more memorable.

The Committee of Safety in February 1775 ordered the commanders of the town militias to assemble one-quarter of their men and to occupy and hold a long list of vital points of communication and

---

383 *American Archives*. Peter Force, ed. 9 vols. in series IV and V. Washington D.C.: Government Printing Office, 1837-1853. Series 4, Volume 1, p. 1046. Hereinafter cited as *Amer Arch,* with series number given first, volume second and page number last.

384 *London Chronicle, 21 January 1775; 2 February 1775.*

security. On 28 June this list was expanded and the Committee created twenty-three militia companies of fifty men each to guard the seacoast and to watch for English naval activities. By January 1776 the militia was ordered to form eight additional companies to guard coastal locations not covered by the first order.[385]

The militia supplies at Salem were moved to what the Committee of Safety thought were more secure quarters at Concord. The Congress resolved that any time the British high command moved five hundred or more of its troops out of Boston this act would be considered to be hostile to the colony. The Congress authorized the Committee of Safety to act in defense of the colony and its citizens. Force against a large troop deployment was automatically defined as a defensive act. There was no authorization of offensive action.

On 15 April 1775 General Gage acted. He issued orders to his elite troops, men especially selected out of all regular army units under Gage's command. They were to train for a search and destroy mission. The command extended to over seven hundred select men. The Committee of Safety and Massachusetts Congress watched and waited. The British reported that on the eighteenth of April the following companies were committed to action: "the grenadiers of his army and the light infantry, under the command of Lieutenant-Colonel Smith of the Tenth Regiment, and Major Pitcairn, of the Marines . . . and the next morning eight companies of the Fourth and the same number of the Twenty-third and Forty-ninth, and some marines, marched under the command of Lord Percy to support the other detachment."[386]

On the night of 18 April 1775 Paul Revere and William Dawson received word. They must cross Boston harbor, past H. M. S. Somerset, and prepared to spread the alarm. Revere, a Boston silversmith, had been responsible for the popular copperplate depicting the colonists' view of the Boston Massacre of 5 March 1770. He was a trusted courier for the Committee of Safety and had arranged to set in motion a warning system should the British authorities decide to

---

385 Greenough, C. P., "How Massachusetts Raised her Troops in the Revolution," *Collections of the Massachusetts Historical Society*, 55 (1921-22), p. 348.
386 "The British Account of the Battles of Lexington and Concord, White Hall, June 15, 1775," in *American Museum, or, Repository of Ancient and Modern Fugitive Pieces, Etc.* Philadelphia: Matthew Carey. 1789, 5: 87. See also Franklin B. Hough. *The Day of Lexington and Concord, the 19th of April 1775*. Little Brown, 1925.

move against the revolutionary leaders. Dr. Joseph Warren, chair of the Massachusetts Committee of Safety, ordered Revere to issue the warning, saying that the British troops were preparing to march from Boston. Using a small rowboat he had secreted, Revere avoided detection by British naval patrols. He borrowed a horse in Charlestown and set out for Concord. Initially blocked by British patrols along the Cambridge Road, Revere rode through Medford, arriving at about midnight at Lexington. At the home owned by Reverend Jonas Clarke, Revere awakened John Hancock and Samuel Adams. Warren had also sent William Dawes to Roxbury. Joined by Dr Samuel Prescott of Concord, Revere and Dawes set out to spread the alarm along the whole line of communities in which Minutemen were awaiting news of British movements, especially those guarding the militia supplies at Concord. Intercepted by a British patrol, Revere was captured, Dawes fled back toward Lexington, but Prescott escaped to carry the message to Lincoln and Concord. Revere convinced his captors that the entire countryside was already alarmed and gathering under arms and they would be at great risk in holding him. The British officer in charge released Revere who then returned to Lexington and there rescued vital papers that Hancock had left behind. There he saw the first shots fired.

Samuel Adams and John Hancock authorized the sounding of the general alarm. For the next sixteen hours the militia responded. Lexington awakened, the word spread toward Concord. Through the night as the British column moved forward, news of their march was eliciting a colonial response. The quick trip across the Charles River in boats was the easy part for the British troops. They disembarked into knee deep cold water. Then they assembled at arms for two hours. They marched waist deep through the biting cold of a backwater. As they marched northward they became aware that surprise was not their ally. Church bells and other sounds of the night served notice that their mission was uncovered. In command was Colonel Francis Smith of the Tenth Lincolnshires. Second in command was Marine Major John Pitcairn. If not the senior commander at least his second inspired confidence.

Daylight began to break as the column neared Lexington. By now the horse hoof beats translated into silhouettes of horse and rider. The sound of the ringing bells translated into armed men gathering informally into armed units. "The country had been much alarmed,"

Gage reported, "By the firing of guns and ringing of bells." He then dispatched two companies to secure two important bridges.[387] The semi-lit fields seemed to be filled with human beings headed toward their rendez-vous with destiny. Pitcairn dispatched a messenger to Gage in Boston. He told of the premature discovery of his mission and asked for additional troops.

As the column entered Lexington they saw before them two companies of Minutemen. Battle order was formed on the close end of the town green. There was no surprise, only discomfort at the approaching moment of decision. Captain John Parker of Lexington sized up the situation correctly. The first confrontation would not be recorded in Lexington. Gage later reported that his army "found a body of the country people drawn up under arms on a green close to the road; and upon the king's troops marching up to them, in order the enquire the reason of their being so assembled, they went off in great confusion." Pitcairn wanted no battle for his part either. But his orders were clear. All militia under arms were to be detained and disarmed and/or taken into custody. Pitcairn turned his column to cut off the retreat of the militia. A shot rang out. No one save the person who pulled the trigger will ever know who bears the responsibility for the start of the war. Gage reported it was probably the Americans who fired first. "Several guns were fired upon the kings' troops from behind a stone wall and also from the meeting house, and other houses, by which one man was wounded, and major Pitcairn's horse shot in two places."[388]

After the first anonymous shot the British line fired in volleys. The troops broke rank and charged the militiamen. Pitcairn struggled to restore order and stop the firing. Eight Americans lay dead on the Lexington green. There were no remarkable British casualties. The column reformed and marched on toward Concord and the military supplies stored there. Reuben Brown, saddler of Concord, had ridden to Lexington for news. He returned to report to the colonials that the British had fired on the militia at Lexington. The militia readied itself for the British troops. The militia at Concord had received reinforcements. The Lincoln militia had arrived and advance notice was received that yet other militia units were due to arrive momentarily. The militia marched out to meet the British troops and escorted them

---

387 Gage, quoted in *American Museum*, p. 87.
388 Gage, quoted in *American Museum*, p. 87.

into the village. The citizen-soldiers occupied the high ground beyond their muster field. The British began to ransack the town. The militia from Acton, Carlisle and Chelmsford arrived, swelling the colonial ranks. Captain Isaac Davis, the gunsmith, spotted smoke arising for the town and concluded that the British were burning the town. He led his Acton militia in the charge and the battle was engaged.

This time there was no doubt who fired first. The British loosed volley after volley. Davis had made his last gun, for he was probably the first to fall to the British troops at Concord. The streets turned into slaughter pens. The militia ignored military formation so familiar to the disciplined English troops. They fanned out and fired not in volleys but on individual initiative at selected targets. Their aimed precision drove the best of Gage's command back. The lines broke and the English fled in disarray. Back to Lexington they raced.

The account of the action was published in a local newspaper and was widely reprinted for weeks after in nearly all the newspaper in other areas of the nation. This American account claimed the British commander cried,

> "Disperse you Rebels -- Damn you! Throw down your Arms and dispense." Upon which the Troops huss'd, and immediately one or two Officers discharged their Pistols, which were instantaneously followed by the Firing of four or five of the Soldiers,then there seemed to be a general discharge from the whole Body.[389]

There are a number of extant depositions taken from Americans who witnessed the massacre. They differ slightly in the report of the exact words spoken by the British commander, and whether it was the commander or his lieutenant who gave the order to fire. For example, Elijah Sanderson claimed that he was present on Lexington common and he "heard one of the regulars say, 'damn them, we will have them' and immediately the regulars shouted aloud, ran and fired upon the Lexington company." Simon Winthrop "observed an officer at the head of the said troops, flourishing his sword, and with a loud voice, giving the word, 'fire -- fire' which was instantly followed by a discharge of arms." John Parker, commander of the Lexington militia, claimed that "I immediately ordered our militia to disperse and not to fire." The "regular troops were on the march from Boston, in order to

---

[389] *Essex Gazette,* 25 April 1775.

take the province stores at Concord" and upon his order not to fire the British "troops made their appearance and rused furiously, fired upon and killed eight of our party." A number of members of Parker's militia signed a common affidavit,[390] which claimed that "about five o'clock in the morning, hearing our drum beat we proceeded toward the parade" grounds where they formed. Seeing that "a large body troops were marching toward us" they heard orders from Parker to offer no resistance." At which time the company began to disperse. Whilst our backs were turned on the troops, we were fired on by them, and a number of our men were instantly killed." Levi Mead and Levi Harrington reported that "two of the regulars whom took to be officers, fired a pistol or two on the Lexington company, which was dispersing, and they were immediately followed by several vollies from the regulars."

    William Draper reported that "the commanding officer, as I took him, gave the command to fire upon the said troops, 'fire, fire, fire' and immediately they fired before any of captain Parker's company fired." Thomas Fessenden gave this account. "I saw three officers on horseback advance to the front of the said regulars, when one of them, being within six rods of the said militia, cried out, 'disperse you rebels, immediately,' on which he brandished his sword over his head three times; meanwhile the second officer, who was about two rods behind him, fired a pistol, pointed at said militia, and the regulars kept huzzaing till he had finished brandishing his sword, and when he had thus finished brandishing his sword, he pointed it down toward the said militia, and immediately on which, the said regulars fired a volley at the militia." After the initial shots were fired "the said militia dispersed every way as fast as they could and while they were dispersing, the regulars kept firing at them incessantly."[391]

---

390 Signers included: Nathaniel Mulliken, Philip Russell, Moses Harrington, Jr., Thomas and David Harrington, William Grimes, William Tidd, Isaac Hastings, Jonas Stone, Jr., James Wyman, Thaddeus Harrington, John Chandler, Joshua Reed, Jr., Joseph Symonds, Phineas Smith, John Chandler, Jr., Reuben Cock, Joel Viles, Nathan Reed, Samuel Tidd, Bejamin Lock, Thomas Winship, Simeon Snow, John Smith, Moses Harrington III, Joshua Reed, Ebenezer Parker, John Harrington, Enoch Willington, John Hormer, Isaac Green, Phineas Stearn, Isaac Durant and Thomas Headley, Jr.

391 These and other depositions were first published in *American Museum,* or *Repository of Ancient and Modern Fugitive Pieces, Etc.* Philadelphia: Matthew Carey, 1789, 5: 79-87.

Meanwhile, several companies of British troops which had moved beyond the town returned. They had seen and heard the battle at the bridge. As they returned the militia covered them, but did not fire. The citizen-soldiers seemed willing to avoid further hostilities if possible. Colonel Smith assembled his Lincolnshire companies. They could see ever more militiamen arriving. They seemed to be aware that news of the two bloody confrontations was spreading among the new arrivals. As they finally left town at about high noon the British fired a parting volley at the militia. This act of contempt was the immediate cause of the Battle of the Nineteenth of April 1775.

The citizen-soldiers knew better than to attempt to fight the British regulars on their own terms. They did not form a line of attack. They hid behind rocks and trees, behind fences, wood piles and outbuildings. They fired, retreated, reloaded and fired again. Gage reported that "on the return of the troops from Concord, they were very much annoyed, and had several men killed and wounded, by rebels firing from behind walls, ditches, trees and other ambushes. " The British troops that were put to flight by the citizen-soldiers of Massachusetts were quite probably the finest in the world. But they had retreated Many threw away their weapons and back packs and ran. As the harried British troops arrived back in Lexington, at the sight of the first blood, they were joined by some two thousand fresh troops under Lord Percy. Percy had recruited three loyalist guides from Boston: Thomas Beaman of Petersham; Samuel Murray of Brookfield; and Edward Winslow, Jr., of Plymouth.[392] The early morning call for assistance had been answered.

But the calm was short lived. Percy brought several small cannon and fired at the Americans with these. Gage reported, "the rebels were for a while dispersed; but as soon as the troops resumed their march, they began to fire upon them again from behind stone walls and houses, and kept up in that manner a scattering fire during the whole of their march of 15 miles, by which means several were killed and wounded." As the combined forces returned to Boston they found the citizen-soldiers were positioned along the road just as they had been with the smaller column. They were bold in their harassment. Occasionally, the column stopped to fire back or to set up light

---

392 Siebert, William H., "Loyalist Troops of New England," *New England Quarterly,* 4 (1931), pp. 108-47.

artillery wherewith to sweep the colonial lines. But the muskets were highly inaccurate at the distance between the column on the road and the colonials in their hiding places. There were seldom enough men concentrated to justify the use of even the small artillery pieces in the British command.

Although Gage had twice reported only that "several" men were killed or wounded, the British suffered seventy-two killed and many more wounded on that fateful day. Gage even reported that "such was the cruelty and barbarity of the rebels that they scalped and cit off the ears of some of the wounded men."[393] Superior marksmanship and the use of rifles rather than the New England fowling pieces would have inflicted even more casualties. These were not backwoodsmen or hunters whose lives depended upon proper and accurate use of their guns. They were merchants, tradesmen, clergymen and farmers who had far less experience with aimed, precision firing than had their backwoods cousins. Moreover, their fowling pieces were not rifled arms.[394] One American wrote to an English newspaper that "had the people had time to have alarmed the country, and to have collected their militia, it is probable that the retreat of the regulars would have been totally cut off."[395] Perhaps the most significant fact noted about this engagement was that the Massachusetts militia had turned out no less than 3763 Americans even though the patriots had received only a few hours' notice.

A few days after the incidents, General Gage appeared before the Selectmen of Boston. He reported that "there was a large body of men in arms" and that he was prepared to take whatever action was necessary to maintain might be injured in any resulting confrontation.[396] The patriots claimed that "20 or 30 thousand men . . . surrounded Boston and shut in the British soldiers and cut off all supplies of fresh provisions."[397] Gage demanded that the inhabitants give up their arms and place them, with tags denoting individual ownership attached thereunto, in a public hall in Boston. Later, "the arms afore-

---

393 Gage in *American Museum*, 87.
394 Fowling pieces were designed to fire pellets like a modern shotgun although they were safe for use with a single ball. At distances greater than fifty yards they were not especially accurate and were comparable to the British muskets. They were by far the most common firelock in Massachusetts.
395 *Bristol Gazette*, 24 August 1775.
396 *Connecticut Courant,* 17 July 1775.
397 *Bristol Gazette*, 24 August 1775.

said at a "suitable time" would be return'd to the owners."[398] The inhabitants did bring in 1778 firearms, 634 pistols, 973 bayonets and 38 blunderbusses.[399]

Boston became an armed camp. Patriots bragged that the "militia at present consists of 17 or 20 thousand men" all under "strict military discipline plus another "20 or 30 thousand farmers who hold themselves ready to march at a minute's warning." In short, "all the yeomanry are under arms as a militia."[400] Reports of the militia spontaneously rising were received from as far away as Virginia. There, reports of the events at Lexington and Concord had spurred the people into preparedness.

> We shall therefore in a few weeks have about 8000 volunteers (about 1500 of which are horse) all completely equipped at their own expence, and you may depend are as ready to face death in defence of their civil and religious liberty as any men under heaven. These volunteers are but a small part of our militia; we have in the whole about 100,000 men. The New England provinces have at this day 50,000 of as well trained soldiers as any in Europe, ready to take the field at a day's warning, it is as much as the more prudent and moderate among them can do, to prevent the more violent from crushing General Gage's little army. But I still hope there is justice and humanity, wisdom and sound policy, sufficient in the British nation to prevent the fatal consequences that must inevitably follow the attempting to force by violence the tyrannical acts of which we complain. It must involve you in utter ruin, and us in great calamities, which I pray heaven to avert, and that we may once more shake hands in cordial affection as we have hitherto done, and as brethren ought ever to do. . . . Messrs. Hancock and Adams passed through this city a few days ago . . . about 1000 of our inhabitants went out to meet them, under arms . . . . By last accounts from Boston, there were before the town 15,000 or 20,000 brave fellows to defend their country, in high spirits . . . . Should the King's troops attack, the inhabitants will be joined with 70,000 or 80,000 men at very short notice. . . .[401]

The news of Lexington reached Philadelphia about five o'clock in the afternoon on Monday, 24 April 1775, from Trenton, New

---

398 *Connecticut Courant,* 23 April 1775.
399 Frothingham, R. *History of the Siege of Boston.* Little, Brown, 1903, p. 95.
400 *Bristol Gazette,* 24 August 1775.

401 Letter from Virginia, 16 April 1775, *London Chronicle,* 1 June 1775.

Jersey.[402] Reprints of more northerly newspapers appeared for several days in Virginia and South Carolina.

The English press at first discounted the possibility of real and open rebellion, preferring to think that the skirmishes were acts of isolated insolence.[403] By mid-July the English press was reporting that "the Town of Boston was surrounded by a large body of Rebel Provincials and that all communication with the Country was cut off." An American correspondent of a London newspaper reported that all New England was an armed camp.

> Several companies of New England men are actually arrived in this town [New York]. I conversed with one of them, who told me he had left his farm to come to our assistance; and one of their Captains assured our people, that if they wanted men, they could furnish us with ten thousand in three days time. They exercise to admiration: it is true they have not that sprightly and foppish appearance of regular forces when nicely powdered; however, they are hardy, can endure fatigue, and have made themselves masters of the essential parts of military skill. Four New England governments have two hundred thousand of these soldiers in arms; they are a sober, good kind of people, strong pedestrians, and think it a part of their religious duty to defend their charters . . . .[404]

Things in Boston after the conflict at Concord went from bad to worse. Gage accused some Bostonians of being incendiaries andhings in Boston after the conflict at Concord went from bad to worse. Gage accused some Bostonians of being incendiaries and ordered that "all Persons. . . should immediately lay down their arms" and desist from "burning houses." In Charles Town some three hundred and fifty houses burned in one night. Gage let it be known that the king was still willing to pardon all rebels except John Adams and John Hancock. On 17 May a fire broke out and "it was the officers order not to call fire, one having threatened to beat out a man's brains that did."[405] A letter from Charles Town dated 19 May 1775 noted that Gage "agreed, on delivering up their arms, they should come out with their effects." Unfortunately for the colonists, "it is complied with on their part; on his there is a shocking failure."[406] The British marines

---

402 A facsimile of that original message was reproduced in *Pennsylvania Magazine of History and Biography*, 27 [1903]: following page 257.
403 *London Gazette*, 30 May 1775.
404 *Morning Chronicle and London Advertiser*, 5 July 1775.
405 A letter from Boston, *London Evening Post*, 26 June 1775.
406 Letter from Charles Town, New England, 19 May 1775, *Lloyd's Evening Post*

had little respect for the militiamen whom they had easily dispersed. British troops broke into John Hancock's house and "plundered" his possessions and also the same night began to "pillage and break down" the fences of other homes.[407] Meanwhile, "the first Embarkation of Troops from Ireland, consisting of three Regiments of Infantry and one of Light Cavalry, was arrived at Boston" and would quickly disperse the rebels.[408]

> [A] body of the king's troops . . . were secretly landed at Cambridge, with an apparent design to take or destroy the military and other stores, provided for this colony, and deposited at Concord -- that some inhabitants of the colony . . . travelling peacefully on the road . . . were seized and greately abused by armed men...that the regular troops on their way to Concord, marched into the said town of Lexington, and the said [militia] company, on their approach, began to disperse -- that, notwithstanding this, the regulars rushed on with great violence and first began hostilities, by firing on said Lexington company, whereby they killed eight, and wounded several others -- that the regulars continued their fire, until those of the said company, who were neither killed or wounded had made their escape -- that . . . the detachment then marched to Concord, where a number of provincials were again fired on by the troops, two of them killed and several wounded, before the provincials fired on them.... To give a particular account of the ravages of the troops, as they retreated from Concord to Charlestown, would be difficult. . . .[409]

One of the earliest clashes between Massachusetts militia nd British forces occurred immediately after the British march on Lexington and Concord, just off a neck of land near Boston Harbor. A band of militia, calling themselves "true sons of liberty," challenged the seamen aboard the Lively Frigate on 20 April at about five o'clock in the morning. Both sides exchanged shots from both muskets and small swivel guns loaded with grape shot. A British sailor on the ship reported, "The Americans had 25 killed and 30 wounded, whom they left on shore." American fire "killed two and wounded many more."

---

and British Chronicle, 28 June 1775.
407 Letter from Worcester, Massachusetts Bay, 20 May 1775, *London Chronicle*, 8 July 1775.
408 *London Gazette*, 18 July 1775.
409 "Report of the Massachusetts Provincial Congress, or, Address by the Massachusetts Provincial Congress, sitting at Watertown, to the Inhabitants of Great Britain," [26 April 1775] in Alden T. Vaughan, ed. *Chronicles of the American Revolution*. Columbia University Press, 1965, p. 167.

After exchanging fire for about an hour, "we sailed for Boston with colours flying."[410]

Leaving no doubt as to the cause of the conflict between the colonies and the mother nation, on 6 July 1775, representatives from Massachusetts introduced to the Continental Congress a document drafted by Thomas Jefferson and John Dickinson, the "Declaration of the Causes and Necessity of Taking up Arms." The document described how General Gage's troops disarmed the compliant citizen-soldiers of Boston.

> The inhabitants of Boston being confined within that town by the general their governor, and having, in order to procure their dismission, entered into a treaty with him, it was stipulated that the said inhabitants having deposited their arms with their own magistrates, should have liberty depart, taking with them their other effects. They accordingly delivered up their arms, but in open violation of honour, in defiance of the obligation of treaties, which even savage nations esteemed sacred, the governor ordered the arms deposited as aforesaid, that they might be preserved for their owners, to be seized by a body of soldiers; detained the greatest part of the inhabitants of the town, and compelled the few who were permitted to retire, to leave their most valuable effects behind. By this perfidy wives are separated from their husbands, children from their parents, and the aged and sick from their relations and friends, who wish to attend and comfort them, and those who have been used to live in plenty and even elegance, are reduced to deplorable distress.[411]

The French press reacted with delight upon receiving the news of the commencement of hostilities in Massachusetts Bay. It referred to the English as "tyrants" and expressed pleasure that the conflict had turned bloody.[412] The French reported that the militia "breathed the same courage, the same desire of defending their rights and their liberties... to the last individual."[413] The Press reported that women were joining the militia. It reported a company of "Amazons" who had "taken up arms to second their husbands in defense of their rights."[414]

---

410 Letter from a midshipman on board the *Lively Frigate* now stationed off the neck of land near Boston, *London Morning Post and Daily Advertiser*, 13 July 1775. The midshipman reported that the date of the action was 20 April, but his letter was dated 14 May. 1775.
411 *Documents Illustrative of the Formation of the Union of American States*. 69th Congress, 1st Session, H.R. Doc. 398 [1927], pp.14-15.
412 *Gazette des Deux-Ponts*, 12 June 1775.
413 *Gazette de Leyde*, 4 July 1776.
414 *Gazette des Deux-Ponts,* 27 July and 24 August 1775; *Gazette de France*, 25

And it relayed tales of citizen-soldiers performing impossible feats, such as militiamen firing, reloading and firing at a rate of eleven shots per minute.[415] The French perceived our militia as invincible.

The Battle of Bunker Hill followed the British occupation of Boston. During May 1775 both the Americans and the British had built up their strength around Boston. Three British general arrived to assist Gage, Sir William Howe (1729-1814), Sir Henry Clinton (1738-1795), and John Burgoyne (1722-1792). On 12 June Gage offered amnesty to all rebels except Samuel Adams and John Hancock, placed the city under martial law and declared all rebels under arms to be traitors. Learning that Gage planned to fortify Dorchester Heights, the Massachusetts Council of War ordered the militia to build fortifications on Bunker Hill, later changed to Breed's Hill, overlooking Boston Harbor from Charlestown peninsula.

On 17 June Gage discovered the Americans and ordered his ships in the harbor to begin to shell their position. After the tide was correct for landing, Gage ordered his troops to disembark and commerce a frontal assault on the American position. The official American version of the battle described the way the patriots waited on the British troops before firing. "The provincials within their entrenchments impatiently waited the attack of the enemy and reserved their fire till they came within 10 or 12 rods, and then began a furious discharge of small arms." The militia repeated this tactic during the second and third British charge.[416] General Howe moved twenty-four hundred troops into the battle, but withering fire from the militia twice drove them back. If not before, one can easily trace the mystique of the unerring colonial rifleman to this battle for the dead shots picked off British officers virtually at will.

Reinforced by Clinton, Howe ordered a bayonet charge which routed the militia commanded by Colonel William Prescott and Dr. Joseph Warren.[417] Warren was killed as were 100 other Americans,

---

August 1775.
415 *Gazette des Duex-Ponts,* 19 December 1774.
416 "An Account of the Battle of Bunker's Hill, published by a committee of the Provincial Congress of Massachusetts," in *American Museum, or, Repository of Ancient and Modern Fugitive Pieces, Etc.* Philadelphia: Matthew Carey, 1789, 5: 107.
417 A long and glowing eulogy to Dr. Warren is found in "An Eulogium on the memory of the major general Warren who fee June 17, 1775, at Bunker's Hill,

with 276 wounded and 30 taken prisoner. British losses were staggering, with 1054 report casualties, or 42% of the British troops engaged. Moreover, American marksmen concentrated their fire on the officer corps and a large proportion of those killed were commissioned officers.[418] The British stopped at the end of peninsula and several days later General George Washington arrived to take supreme command.

The Siege of Boston was an eleven month period which began on 19 April 1775, following the incidents at Lexington and Concord, and ending on 17 March 1776, when the British withdrew. The Patriot militia, supported by thousands of volunteers from the other colonies, surrounded British forces, confining them to the city and its immediate environs. When the Patriots placed cannon, obtained from Fort Ticonderoga, on the heights above the city, the British capitulated, ending the siege. Thereafter, the Massachusetts militia was called upon to perform few functions beyond acting as a reservoir of manpower for the Continental Line.[419]

---

written shortly after that lamented event, in *American Museum*, 5: 200-02. Some thought that, had Warren lived, he might have become supreme commander of American forces, or at least one of the Continental Army's most important commanders.

418 French, Allen. *The First Year of the American Revolution*. New York: Octagon, 1934; and Richard Frothingham. *History of the Siege of Boston*. Boston: Little Brown, 1849.

419 Barbier, Brooke. *Boston in the American Revolution: A Town Versus an Empire*. Arcadia Publishing, 2017.

Militia Law during the Revolution

There was no Patriot standing army in Massachusetts when the Revolution began; neither had there been in any colony a regular full-time army in any province. All colonies relied fully and completely upon their respective militia organizations. All able-bodied men were more or less enrolled in militia companies, about thirty in all, with companies ranging in size from between two hundred to seven hundred men each. The militiamen were divided into two classes. The active list encompassed all able-bodied males between ages sixteen and fifty. There were many exemptions from this enrollment on this list, including religious leaders and conscientious objectors, civil officers and others engaged in vital occupations, such as arms makers and ferry operators. This list was supplemented by the alarm list which included all males between sixteen and sixty-five not enrolled on the active list.

There were few exemptions from this list for it was to be used only in cases of extreme emergency at such time as all available men who could fight had to be mustered. This list was of significance when an enemy attacked during a period when most, if not all, regular militiamen were absent from town. The active list mustered eight times a year for training lasting from three to seven days at each muster, and the alarm list was supposed to muster twice a year, although it complied with the law so only on rare occasion. General officers of each list were appointed by civil authorities, but the non-commissioned officers and officers inferior to full colonel were elected as had been traditional. The musters rarely produced much real military training in the sense of a European army of the time.

Following the orders of Congress, in the fall of 1775, the legislature of Massachusetts enacted a new militia law. Generally, the militia itself was not deployed outside Massachusetts and there was only sporadic action within the state. The colony was ordered to provide each inhabitant with a good musket. Public officers were to arrange to collect arms from private holders and to distribute these to such of the militia men who had none of their own. Those militia men who brought their own arms were to receive a bounty of ten shillings.[420]

---

420 4 *American Archives* 2: 1018-20.

On 16 January 1776 the Massachusetts General Council ordered men between the ages sixteen and fifty years of age be enrolled in the militia, provide their own weapons under penalty of law, elect their own officers and muster and train several times a year.[421] It also resolved that "free Negroes who have served faithfully in the Army at Cambridge may be reenlisted therein, but no others."[422]

The armed force of the state, and of the nation, at this point consisted solely of volunteers drawn from the militia; and of the militia, in various sub-divisions. The volunteers were treated in exactly the same way as the militia, receiving only basic subsistence pay. The men provided their own weapons, clothing, accoutrements and supplies. Massachusetts allowed the men $4 each for overcoats during the winter of 1775-76. There was not as yet any realization among the men that a prolonged struggle lay before them. As at the beginning of any way, men were overcome by sentiments of patriotism and spurred to action by propaganda efforts, such as Thomas Paine's The Crisis and the Declaration of Independence.

During the early years of the Revolution, the members of the Continental Army in Massachusetts were largely drawn from volunteers among the active list, as was the case in all states The active list militiamen often fought as units in the first months of the Revolution, and intermittently thereafter. As the war continued, volunteers, and even impressments through state drafts, drew almost equally on the two lists. By 1780 the distinction between the lists had become so blurred that there was no longer an attempt made of keeping the lists separate. Colonels of the militia, often referred to as county lieutenants, enjoyed considerable latitude in drafting men for service in the Continental Line, or assigning men to various other duties. The principal limitation on military commanders was demographic. State law in Massachusetts, as in most New England states, required that levees be assigned according to the population of the various towns and districts. After the British evacuated Boston there was little for the militia to do except come to the aid of its neighbors, notably Rhode Island and New York.[423]

On 21 April 1775 the Committee of Safety voted to raise eight

---

421 *Acts and Resolves, Public and Private, of the Province of Massachusetts Bay.* Boston: State of Massachusetts, 1869-1922, 5: 445-54.
422 4 *American Archives* 4: 1644.
423 Greenough, C. P., "How Massachusetts Raised Her Troops in the Revolution," *Collections of the Massachusetts Historical Society*, 60 (1921-22), pp. 345-70.

thousand volunteers from among the militia to serve for seven months. Two days later the Provincial Congress increased the authorization to include 13,600 men. Ultimately, the colony decided that a force of thirty thousand men, including all active forces and reserve militia. The militia was divided into three classes: the Minutemen, who were to respond immediately to any threat from British or Amerindian threats; the regular militia, who acted as back-up forces and a reserve from which to draw volunteers, and, later on, as a reservoir for the state drafts; and the invalid corps of those who, through injury, infirmity or age, could not serve in ordinary circumstances, but which constituted a final line of defense.[424]

As it was, Massachusetts actually raised seventeen thousand men in 1775. The Committee of Safety chose the principal officers and the men elected their officers inferior to full colonel. In May 1775 the Committee ordered two thousand volunteers to report to Boston to assist in lifting the siege, and it ordered the towns to muster and hold in indefinite reserve one-half of the active militia. The Committee was not prepared to feed, clothe, house and otherwise provide for a greater number in and around Boston, but wished to have a larger force available immediately in case of major military action with the British. The force sent to Boston, along with militia, volunteers and others from Connecticut, New Hampshire and Rhode Island fought the Battle of Bunker Hill on 17 June 1775.[425]

On 21 January 1776 the state legislature authorized the recruitment of 728 volunteers, to be drawn primarily from the militias of Hampshire and Berkshire counties, to serve in Canada. The militia was clearly not authorized to march beyond the border of the new nation. There were some questions about the deployment of militia in other states, although mutual aid pacts and traditional understandings seemed to grant full authorization for deployment of Massachusetts militia within the rest of the New England states. Deployment of the militia in New York, New Jersey, Pennsylvania or elsewhere was of questionable legality. But there was no question that volunteers would have to be drawn for any service outside the United Colonies, just as volunteers had been drawn for British service against the French over the previous century. The militia was the principal, but

---

[424] *Massachusetts Soldiers and Sailors in the Revolutionary War*, I: xii.

[425] *Massachusetts Soldiers and Sailors in the Revolutionary War*, I: xiv.

not sole, source of volunteers. The legislature offered a bounty of 40 shillings to each volunteer. Service and payments were authorized for one year's service, 21 January 1776 through 1 January 1777.[426]

Early in 1776 the Massachusetts legislature enacted a new militia law, thereby repealing all previous acts. Appointment of general and field officers became the provenance of the state legislature. The militia encompassed all males. It was divided into two classes, the active and the alarm lists. The alarm list was comprised of those who would serve as minutemen, ready and able to go into action immediately upon notice of an emergency. Regardless of class, each man was required to provide himself, at his own expense, with a suitable firearm; priming wire and brush; bayonet, sword, hatchet or tomahawk; knife; tow for wadding; canteen; knapsack; blanket; and ammunition. Theoretically, a man could plead extreme poverty and expect to have the selectmen of the town provide him with such equipment as he could not afford.[427]

Each man was theoretically responsible for providing his own arms, ammunition, accoutrements and equipment. The selectmen of the community were supposed to make provision for arming the poor, but did so only occasionally. There was no uniformity of bore or caliber of the arms, so providing standard ammunition was essentially impossible. The most that could be done was to provide bar lead from which the men cast their own bullets and kegs of gunpowder from which men made cartridges or filled their powder horns. There were no uniforms, with most militiamen wearing much the same clothing that they wore at home.

Black militiamen presented a problem for the Massachusetts militia. Initially, the colony had enlisted free blacks, which effectively meant any person of color since only a very few slaves were maintained there. In 1775 General George Washington expressed his preference that no "stroller, Negro or vagabond" be enlisted.[428] On 20 May 1775 the Massachusetts Council of Safety "resolved that ... no slaves shall be admitted into this army upon any consideration" and refused free blacks on the ground their admission would be "inconsistent with the procedures that are to be supported" meaning that they would "reflect dishonor on this colony." By the summer 1777 several

---

426 *Acts and Resolves of the Massachusetts Assembly*, 19: 221.
427 *Acts and Resolves*, 5: 445.
428 Quoted in Otto Lindenmeyer. *Black and Brave*. McGraw Hill, 1970, p. 17.

legislatures in New England began to have second thoughts about cutting off a prime source of strong manpower. Recruits were had to find, so they offered cash bounties to free Afro-Americans and offered freedom to slaves who enlisted and served for their full terms. Urged on by Alexander Hamilton, who favored racially integrated militias, the states found a useful reservoir of manpower within the black community.[429]

For a variety of valid reasons, acceptable firearmss were so scarce that many militiamen, even among those who could afford them, were unable to procure any firearms. The British had confiscated many as we have seen. While militiamen rarely practiced with bayonets, using tomahawks and large knives instead, the Continental Army demanded that shoulder arms have bayonets attached. Fowlers which had been quite acceptable as militia arms, were wholly unsuited for use with bayonets. Early militia acts had made no attempt to require standardization of caliber; perhaps, regarding fowlers, gauge or bore. In order to prepare cartridges there had to be uniformity in caliber of the small arms. The local committees of safety first confiscated arms from non-associators, which meant from those who refused to sign the new oath of loyalty to the United States. The committees also sought to purchase local citizenry any superfluous arms; and to contract with various tradesmen to manufacture arms.

In early June 1776 the Continental Congress ordered Massachusetts to supply three thousand militia to reinforce the Continental Army then in Canada. Soon after, the Congress requested tow thousand additional militia to march to New York to the relief of the inhabitants there who were under Amerindian attack.[430]

In November 1776 the legislature added to the militia law certain provisions. Patriotism and nationalistic sentiments may have attracted militiamen initially, but the realities of war soon diminished the enthusiasm of all but the most hardy and ardent patriots. A draft became the inevitable alternative. One-quarter of all militiamen were to be designated as potential draftees. Those designated might be selected by lot or marked as prospective draftees at the time of their enlistment. In any event, those drafted could be called up at any time to serve three months with the Continental Line. Short enlistment peri-

---

429 Oliver, Frederick Scott. *Alexander Hamilton*. New York: Crowell, 1970, pp. 74-128.
430 *R. I. Col. Rec.*, 7: 577.

ods constantly hampered the efforts of the regular officers. Those who failed to report for militia duty and musters were subject to moderate fines. Those who had been designated for the draft, and who failed to report within twenty-four hours of notice, could be fined £10 If he failed to report at the time his unit marched off to war he could be fined £12. During his actual service a private was paid £4 per month, with non-commissioned officers paid slightly more. Chronic offenders, and those unable to pay militia fines, could be jailed. Deserters could be punished and even executed upon conviction.[431]

On 20 January 1776 the legislature authorized the enlistment of 4368 men to serve with the Continental Line until 1 April 1776 at the pay of £3 per month. Each town was assigned a quota, to be filled by volunteer militiamen, if possible, and by draft if necessary.[432] In June the legislature authorized the enlistment of five thousand men for the Continental Line from among both the active and the alarm militia lists. Of these five thousand men, three thousand were to be sent to Canada. To attempt to avoid drafting men to serve outside the United Colonies, a bounty of £7 was offered to volunteers. The remaining two thousand men called up were to serve in New York, and to volunteers a bounty of £3 was offered. In both cases, men who provided their own weapons were to be allowed six shillings and twelve shillings for a blanket and supplies.[433] Filling the quota for the Canadian expedition proved to be most difficult so on 12 July the legislature authorized a draft, the first state draft to be used to recruit men to fight on foreign soil. If a man was drafted and refused to march, or to furnish a substitute, he was to be fined £3, with provision made for additional £3 fines.[434]

On 9 July 1776 the legislature authorized two additional regiments for service in Canada. The legislature, noting the previous failure to attract volunteers, immediately moved to a draft, and authorized militia officers to choose every twenty-fifth man from both the regular and alarm militia lists, and notify them of their obligation to serve on the Canadian expedition. Men drafted were to serve until 1 December 1776.[435] In September the legislature ordered that one-fifth of the militia list, regular and alarm, were to be drafted for serve in

---

431 *Acts and Resolves*, 5: 595.
432 *Acts and Resolves*, 39: 217.
433 *Acts and Resolves*, 19: 462, 517.
434 *Acts and Resolves*, 19: 519.
435 *Acts and Resolves*, 19: 517.

New York and New Jersey. This time service was to be "until recalled." Those who failed to report were to be fined £10 and those who failed to march, or to furnish a substitute, were to be fined an additional £10 and jailed.[436] Additional calls for drafts from the militia were made on 30 November, for 90 day service in New York.[437]

As the ranks of the militia were depleted by the several drafts, so the local responsibilities were increased. The militia had sole responsibility for the seacoast watch, for garrisoning various forts and fortified points against both the Amerindians and British forces and protecting vital military stores and manufactories engaged in the production of materials badly needed for the conduct of the war. The Committee of Safety estimated that these responsibilities required the active services of between thirty-five hundred and four thousand militiamen. And, in case of real attack, more militiamen would be required to fight. Some militia were actually enlisted, usually for periods of from thirty to ninety days, to serve at various garrisons and fortresses. Throughout the war the legislature continually resorted to the draft to fill these positions, and, on the average, thirty-five hundred militiamen were on active local duty.[438]

In September 1776 the Continental Congress voted to raise eighty-eight battalions of 726 men each, to constitute a regular army. Enlistments were for the "duration of the war," although it later modified that service, reducing enlistments to three years. Massachusetts was assigned fifteen, later raised to eighteen, regiments.[439] Once again the militia, in both forms, became the source of voluntary recruitment, supplemented quickly by a draft.

States were required to clothe and equip their own quotas, Massachusetts had the right to pick its own uniforms. Massachusetts provided each soldier with two linen hunting shirts, two pairs of pants, a waistcoat made of wool or leather with long sleeves, one pair of breeches, hat of wool or leather, two additional shirts, two pairs of stockings and two pairs or shoes or boots. The state legislature placed a cost of $20 per man of this clothing allowance.[440] It also provide the following arms: a musket with ramrod and bayonet, a worm and priming brush, bayonet scabbard and belt, sword or tomahawk, cartridge

---

436 *Acts and Resolves*, 19: 558.
437 *Acts and Resolves*, 19: 690, 691, 698.
438 Greenough, "Massachusetts Troops," p. 351.
439 *Journals of the Continental Congress*, 2: 336.
440 *Acts and Resolves*, 5: 680-81.

bag or box sufficient to hold 15 rounds of ammunition, 100 swan [or buck] shot, jack-knife, one pound of powder, lead sufficient to make 40 bullets, knapsack, canteen and one blanket.[441] This was substantially the same equipment required of militiamen under the state Militia Act of 1776. In practice, most men brought their own arms and accoutrements, and the state made allowance for such equipment. Men were allowed one penny per mile for travel to the point of rendez-vous, and 20 shillings per month pay for a private.

Massachusetts had an enormously difficult time in filling its initial quota of fifteen regiments, and never did fill the later quota of eighteen regiments. In January 1777 the Committee of Safety and legislature concurred that there was a great need to muster all militiamen so that conscripts to fill the national quota could be located. Thus, the legislature ordered that each county lieutenant or colonel muster his militia company and hold them until the quota was filled. It began by offering an enlistment bounty of £20.[442] Finally, the officers were told to draft every seventh man to fill the regiments.[443]

General Washington asked the state to recruit and equip a battalion of artillery. In March 1777 the legislature offered a bounty of £20 to each recruit for artillery service, although the bounty was reduced to £15/10/0 for those who did not have their own small arms and accoutrements. When the ranks had not been filled by 15 May the legislature authorized the militia officers were to draft enough men to fill the artillery battalion, with service to be only until 10 January 1778. Those failing or refusing to report, or to furnish a substitute, were subjected the rather standard fine of £10, which penalty was increased to one year in jail if the miscreant totally disobeyed the law. This time, the legislature added an additional penalty, a fine of £10, to be levied against the officers and selectmen who failed or refused to follow the law to the letter. Even the handicapped and disabled were required, under the same penalties, to provide substitutes.[444]

By August, the state was still having problems keeping the ranks of the Continental Line filled, so it again called up the militia and increased penalties from £10 to £15. General officers, especially

---
441 *Acts and Resolves*, 5: 448.
442 *Acts and Resolves*, 19: 741.
443 *Acts and Resolves*, 19: 781.
444 *Acts and Resolves*, 19: 141, 781, 821, 921.

those hold the rank of general, were to be dismissed if they failed fill their quotas from among the militia and volunteers. Towns, through their local committees of safety and selectmen, which failed to recruit their full quotas from among the local militia were subject to individual fines of from £4 to £6 per deficiency per month. On 17 April 1778 the legislature, having reached the end of its patience, and under considerable pressure from Congress, ordered that towns which had not filled their quotas were be fined £150 for each man they were short on the date of accounting, set as 20 May 1778. Failures of men to report or provide substitutes were increased on 20 April 1778 to £20. On the same day, fines to be levied against militia officers and town selectmen were also increased to £10 per month for each deficiency. Some of the fines were returned to the towns by offering them bonuses of £30 for each new man recruited by 20 May 1778. As the quotas were filled, the legislature discovered that the drafting of one man out of each seven militiamen was insufficient to raise the numbers needed to fill fifteen regiments. Fifteen hundred additional men were required, so the bounty for volunteers was raised to $300, so as relieve some pressure on the hard-pressed local militia units.[445]

By 9 June 1778 the legislature found it necessary to raise two thousand additional men. To make the enlistment more attractive, the legislature voted to allow conscripts to serve for only nine months instead of the three years that Congress had mandated. Recruiting officers were given a $10 bonus for each new recruit they signed. To sweeten the offer of $300 bounty the state offered 100 acres of land. By volunteers were increasingly difficult to locate, so the draft was reimposed. Men who were, by handicap, age or infirmity, unable to serve had to find substitutes within 24 hours or be assessed a fine of £45, and inability to pay might bring legal action against one's property, goods or estate. Towns which failed to fill their quotas could be assessed a one-time fine of £20 plus £15 per month for each deficiency. Conversely, towns were allowed a bonus of £120 for each new recruit. If the quotas remained unfilled on 1 August 1778, towns could be fined £350 for each deficiency.[446]

On 5 June 1780 the legislature called for 3934 men to serve in the continental line for the term of six months. Any man drafted who refused to report, or who was unfit for duty, had to either furnish a

---
445 *Acts and Resolves*, 20: 367, 386, 415, 702.
446 *Acts and Resolves*, 5: 1297-98; 21: 575.

substitute or be subject to a fine of £150 and possible imprisonment. Pay was 40 shillings a month. It now was payable in silver or gold as an added inducement to join the army for few men were willing to accept the virtually worthless script. Subordinate officers who failed to fill their quotas could be fined up to £100 and commanding officers could be dismissed for similar failings.[447]

By December 1780 the terms of enlistment of those volunteers and draftees from the militia who had been signed in 1776 and 1777 were expiring and additional men were needed to fill the Massachusetts quota. Additionally, desertions, casualties, sickness, injuries and other factors had severely reduced the number of active soldiers. The legislature assigned a state-wide quota of 4240 men, apportioned according to population to the local towns and cities.[448] Under the Act of 2 December 1780,[449] towns were ordered to divide all inhabitants into as many groups as they were short in their quotas, with each group to choose one of its number in any way they chose. If a group failed to produce a man who was acceptable by 31 January 1781, then the town had to hire a man irrespective of cost or inconvenience. Local authorities and town councils were again threatened with fines for failures to fill the ranks. The legislature gave the towns until 31 January 1781 to find the necessary conscripts so again the militia companies were ordered out and a draft imposed.

By law of 26 February 1781 towns were ordered to form their militiamen into as many groups as they were deficient in their quotas for the Continental Line. Each group was responsible for providing on recruit for the army. In cases where the groups of the town militias failed to produce the required recruits, fines were levied and recruitment numbers were increased.[450] This draft was followed by a second draft from the militia completed on 30 June 1781. Towns deficient in filling their quotas by the end of October 1781 were assessed £128/9/6 for each delinquency. In March 1782 the state was still deficient by 1500 men, and the legislature imposed larger quotas on the town militia companies.[451]

Fines, imposed costs, penalties, bonuses, threats and appeals to

---
447 *Acts and Resolves*, 21: 519.
448 *Acts and Resolves*, 21: 38.
449 *Acts and Resolves*, 21: 190.
450 *Acts and Resolves*, 21: 307.
451 *Acts and Resolves*, 21: 190, 621, 656, 825; Greenough, "Massachusetts Troops,", p. 355.

patriotism had all failed miserably to fill the state's quota of soldiers. At the end of the Revolution, Massachusetts reported that it had 4370 active soldiers in national service whereas the state's quota on that date had been 8350 men in continental service.[452] In 1790 Secretary of War Knox reported to Congress that, although Massachusetts and New Hampshire had been assigned a quota of 88 battalions, Massachusetts had never supplied more than 7816 men at a time, that being in 1777. According to General Knox by war's end, Massachusetts had only 3730 men in continental service, or about 600 fewer than the state had previously claimed.[453]

In 1777 as the British force of ten thousand British regulars and Hessian mercenaries under General John Burgoyne prepared to cut the new nation in half with his march from Canada south through New York, there was general alarm sounded throughout New England. The political authorities of the various New England states concluded that this was to be the year that the British would make their major moves. They now had mustered a powerful land force, with regular British troops having been supplemented by Hessian mercenaries. it was uncertain on how many fronts other than New York they might move against.

In January 1777 the Massachusetts legislature created a select militia unit of two thousand militiamen to serve in any of the states of New England until 21 April. In April the Committee of Safety dispatched two companies of militia to march to Rhode Island.[454] On the one hand, the legislature supported the effort by offering a bounty of 20 shillings a month greater bounty than was offered for continental service for marching with the militia; and on the other hand, it provided severe penalties for failing to report as directed.[455] Reports of threatened British and Tory action brought an emergency call, so the militia of the nearest Massachusetts county, Bristol, were ordered to muster and march as soon as possible to Rhode Island until the militiamen ordered out earlier arrived.[456] On 30 April the Committee of safety, with legislative authorization, dispatched fifteen hundred men

---

452 Greenough, "Massachusetts Militia," p. 355.
453 General Knox's report was summarized in Emory Upton. *Military Policy of the United States from 1775*. Washington; U. S. Government Printing Office, 1904, pp. 34, 40, 47, 57-58. Upton particularly disliked trhe militia.
454 *Acts and Resolves*, 19: 765, 877.
455 *Acts and Resolves*, 19: 559, 576, 690.
456 *Acts and Resolves*, 19: 880.

to Fort Ticonderoga, to counter any move Burgoyne's force might make in that direction. The militia units were to serve at the fort for two months.[457]

In May 1777 the legislature authorized the deployment of two regiments of militia at Boston for one year. There was the possibility that these and other militia might have to be deployed elsewhere in New England.[458] The militia resisted, having had its ranks diminished by the drafts to fill the continental line. The legislature countered by offering a $10 bonus to all militiamen who would volunteer for state service before 10 June for the one year term of service. By that date the two regiments, consisting of 1500 militiamen departed for service, which, as it turned out, was to be in Rhode Island.[459] The militiamen were most unhappy at being ordered to serve so far away from their own homes, and in another state. The legislature quickly rescinded the previous order and asked that volunteers be drawn from the two militia regiments to serve "in New England" for a term of two months.[460] On 27 June it changed the term of enlistment from two to six months.[461] The ranks were apparently filled and these militiamen served their full term in Rhode Island.

In July 1777 the officers in charge of the militias of Hampshire and Berkshire Counties, Massachusetts, received orders to muster "all available men" and march to Fort Edward, there to reinforce the northern continental army.[462] On 6 August the legislature sent 2000 militiamen to again reinforce the northern army, but this act was suspended when one-sixth of the militia of seven Massachusetts counties was drafted, to serve until 1 December 1777. The militia called into this service were to be paid £2/10/0 per month.[463]

In September 1777 the legislature ordered that three thousand militia were to be called out immediately for "secret service."[464] In December 1777, the legislature ordered one-half of the militia units of the counties of Middlesex, Worcester, Hampshire and Berskshire, and part of the militia of Essex County, to "join the army" for a one month

---

457 *Acts and Resolves*, 19: 925.
458 *Acts and Resolves*, 19: 931.
459 *Acts and Resolves*, 20: 42.
460 *Acts and Resolves*, 20: 50.
461 *Acts and Resolves*, 20: 52.
462 *Acts and Resolves*, 20: 61.
463 *Acts and Resolves*, 20: 87-88.
464 *Acts and Resolves*, 20: 114.

tour of duty. The militia soon discovered that the primary reason this order had been issued was to draw out the militia and, from it, to recruit volunteers for the continental line. The legislature had authorized payment of a bonus to volunteers of £12/20/0 above the pay offered by the line.[465]

Burgoyne's once fine army surrendered on 17 October 1777, by the Convention of Saratoga. By terms of the agreement, the vast majority of the 5700 prisoners of war were to be taken to Boston, and from there, sent to England, with the proviso that they would not serve again in the war. Responsibility to the care of the prisoners of war fell in large on the Massachusetts militia. Many townspeople were afraid that the prisoners might escape and wreak havoc; and other patriots would have assaulted, possibly murdered, them, on account of real or imagined extra-legal injuries caused by British or Tory forces. The legislature and Committee of Safety authorized the muster of 1000 Massachusetts militia to guard them. In January 1778 the legislature drafted 800 militiamen to serve as guards. It is unclear whether the full compliment of militia had failed to muster or if the militiamen had assumed their tour of duty had expired and went home. In March the legislature issued a third call for militiamen to guard the prisoners. Failure to report for guard duty subjected one to a fine of £10, and one was still considered to be a militiaman and could still be called for guard or other duty immediately after the fine was levied.[466]

In April 1778 the legislature dispatched thirteen hundred Massachusetts militiamen to the defense of the Hudson River. Almost immediately after that deployment, the legislature sent two hundred militiamen to Rhode Island to assist in its defense. Increasingly severe penalties were levied for failures to serve. Even a man inspected and certified physically unfit for military duty had to procure a substitute at his own expense. If a poor invalid was unable to find a volunteer substitute and too destitute to buy one, he might be sent to prison for up to eight months. Moreover, even after an invalid had provided a substitute his name remained on the militia list and he might have to do the same again. Officers had no discretion, and an officer found delinquent, which often meant sympathetic to the plight of a poor man, he might be found guilty of neglect of duty and be fined £30.

---

465 *Acts and Resolves*, 20: 125.
466 *Acts and Resolves*, 20: 191, 255, 333, 470.

The legislature provided a bounty for each man enlisted or drafted of The men were paid the prevailing wages given to privates in the continental line, plus a state bonus of 40 shillings a month.[467]

In 1778 most recruitment effort directed at volunteers, and most deployment of Massachusetts militia, was for service within Rhode Island. In June 1778, Massachusetts sent eighteen hundred militiamen to Rhode Island, to serve for six months. To soften the impact of the order, the legislature paid those called out £4/13/0 a month above the wages received by the continental line. The legislature offered a bonus of £14 for each militiaman sent out of state.[468] On 16 June the legislature sent out two hundred and fifty more militiamen to Rhode Island, to serve only three weeks, until the remainder of eighteen hundred men from the earlier call arrived.[469]

In April 1779 Rhode Island again asked Massachusetts for assistance from its militia. Massachusetts responded by sending out a regiment to serve for eleven months. Pay was £10 above the allowance given by Congress to those serving in the Continental Line. Protests about high taxes, inflation of the state currency and service outside their own state prompted the legislature to increase the allowance to £16 above national wages. Additionally, the legislature offered each man a bounty of £30 and a new suit of clothes. Recruiting officers received a bonus of 30 shillings for each militiaman enlisted. The state still imposed fines and penalties for officers, political officials and men if any man failed to march with his militia regiment.[470] Just three days after the first assignment of militiamen to service in Rhode Island the legislature sent out a call for 500 additional men to march to Rhode Island.[471] On 8 June the legislature ordered 800 militiamen to muster, and assigned them to duty for eight months in Rhode Island. The legislature increased the penalties for failure to report to £30 per incident.[472]

On 26 June 1780 the legislature made an emergency appeal for 4726 volunteer militiamen to enlist for three months' service to march to the Hudson River in New York. Few volunteers were available so a draft ensued. Officers, civil officials and men refusing to march were

---

467 *Acts and Resolves*, 20: 373, 386, 470.
468 *Acts and Resolves*, 20: 441.
469 *Acts and Resolves*, 20: 450.
470 *Acts and Resolves*, 20: 687.
471 *Acts and Resolves*, 20: 694, 700.
472 *Acts and Resolves*, 20: 700; 21: 33.

subjected to fines of up to £300.[473] During the summer of 1780 Massachusetts twice sent militiamen to Rhode Island. In the first case twelve hundred militia were enlisted for forty days' service. Several months later an additional five hundred militiamen were drafted for five months' service.[474]

On 14 December 1780 the selectmen of Grafton submitted a petition to the General Court in Boston, asking that a pension be granted for George Gire, an African-American living in the city. Apparently, Gire had received a pension of 40 shillings per year for his service in the French and Indian War, but, for some reason, it was terminated in June 1779. The selectmen asked that the pension be restored for Gire was aged and infirm and had served his militia well during the war.[475]

On 30 June 1781 the legislature again sent militia into New York, for service on the Hudson River. This time twenty-seven hundred militiamen marched to the defense of West Point. Washington had requested that the militia take the place of some of his regular troops, which regular continental line were dispatched to swell Washington's force at the siege of Yorktown.[476]

The "embattled farmers" who gathered by the "rude bridge" and assembled on the greens at Lexington Green and at Concord on April 19, 1775, embodied perceptions of individual freedom and civil responsibility which had roots in the radical Whigs. During the American Revolution the militia was as much an agent for the spread of patriotism and independence as for acting as a fighting force. Since they were comprised of their neighbors and friends, they helped allay traditional republican fear of standing armies.

---

473 *Acts and Resolves*, 21: 519, 568.
474 *Acts and Resolves*, 21: 324, 625.
475 *Collections of the Massachusetts Historical Society*, 50 (1916-17), pp. 375-411.
476 *Acts and Resolves*, 21: 674.

Thomas Rix (Ricks)

This is one of the earliest known American made firearms known.
Thomas Rix (c.1625-1681)

Pre-Revolutionary War shoulder arm

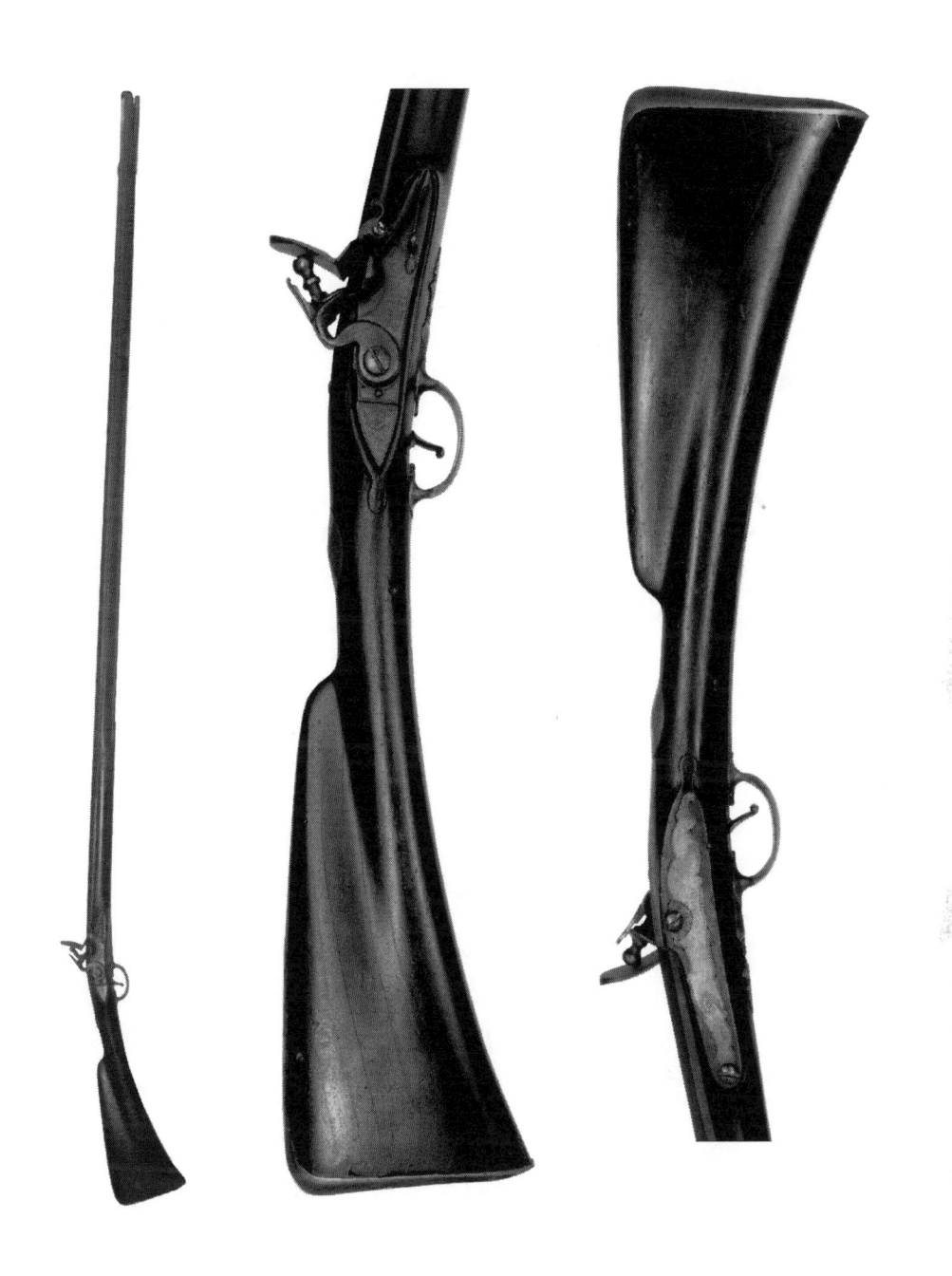

Signed by maker, Horace White (1749-1834)
Early American fowling piece

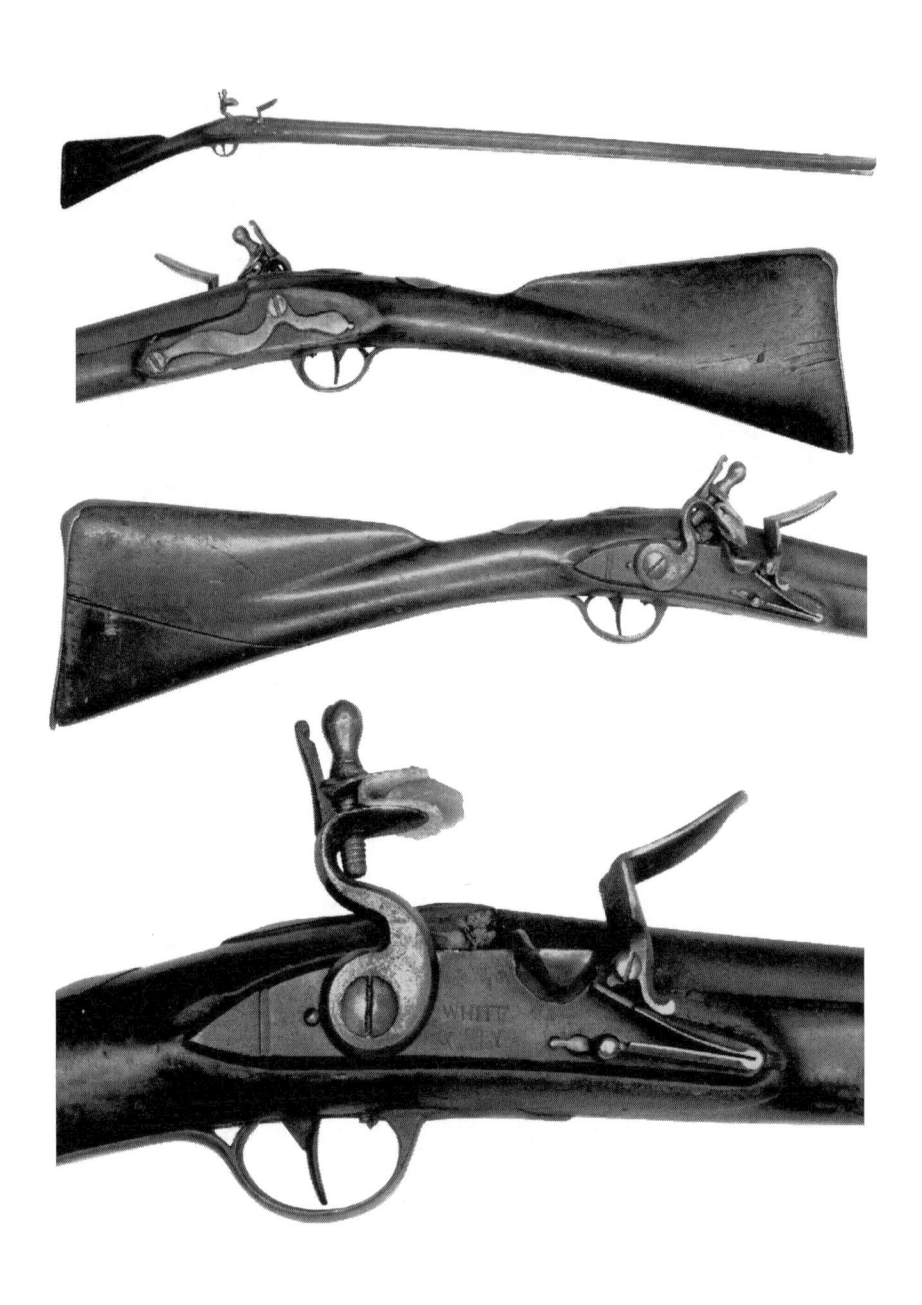

Signed White & Ely
Horace White (1749-1834)
Martin Ely (1741-1822)

Bibliography

Acts and Laws of the General Court of Massachusetts, 1692-1719. London, 1724.

Acts and Resolves, Public and Private, of the Province of Massachusetts. 7 vols. Boston: State of Massachusetts, 1908,

Adams, John. *The Works of John Adams.* Charles F. Adams, ed. 5 vols.. Boston, 1851.

Adams, John Quincy, ed. *The New England Confederacy A Discourse delivered before the Massachusetts Historical Society, at Boston, on the 29th of May 1843; In Celebration of the Second Centennial of that Event.* Charles C. Little and James Brown, 1843.

Agearn, Marie L. *The Rhetoric of War: Training Day, the Militia and the Military Sermon.* Greenwood, 1989.

Alden, John R. *A History of the American Revolution.* Knopf, 1969.

Allen, Zachariah. *Bi-centenary of the Burning of Providence in 1676: Defence of the Rhode Island System of Treatment of the Indians, and of Civil and Religious Liberty. An Address Delivered Before the Rhode Island Historical Society.* Providence Press Company, 10 April 1876.

American Archives. Peter Force, ed. 9 vols. in series IV and V. Washington D.C.: Government Printing Office, 1837-1853. Series never completed.

American Museum, or, Repository of Ancient and Modern Fugitive Pieces, Etc. Philadelphia: Matthew Carey. 1789, 5: 87.

Anderson, Fred. *People's Army: Massachusetts Soldiers and Society in the Seven Years' War.* University of North Carolina Press, 1984,

_____. *Crucible of War: The Seven Years War and the Fate of Empire in British North America, 1754–1766.* Faber and Faber, 2000.

Aspinwall, William, ed. *An Abstract of the Laws of New England as They are Now Established.* London: Aspinwall, 1641.

Bailyn, Bernard. *The Ordeal of Thomas Hutchinson.* Harvard University Press, 1974.

Barbier, Brooke. *Boston in the American Revolution: A Town Versus an Empire.* Arcadia Publishing, 2017.

Barnes, Viola. *Dominion of New England.* Kennikat, 1960.

Barry, Joseph. *History of Massachusetts.* 2 vols. Boston: Philips and Sampson, 1855.

Beattie, Daniel J. "The Adaptation of the British Army to Wilderness Warfare, 1755-1763," in Maarten Ultee. ed. *Adapting to Conditions: War and Society in the Eighteenth Century.* University of Alabama Press, pp. 56-83.

Belknap, Jeremy. *The History of New-Hampshire.* 2 vols. Philadelphia: Robert Aitken, 1784.

Bodge, George M. Bodge. *Soldiers in King Philip's War* Boston: third ed.; Little Brown, 1906.

Boorstin, Daniel. *Americans: The Colonial Experience.* Vintage, 1958.

Boucher, Ronald L., "The Colonial Militia As a Social Institution: Salem, Massachusetts 1764-1775," *Military Affairs,* 37: 4 (1973), pp. 125-130.

Boynton, Lindsay. *The Elizabethan Militia, 1558-1638.* Routledge and Kegan Paul, 1967.

Bradstreet, Howard. *The Story of the War with the Pequots, Retold.* Yale University Press, 1933.

Breen, T. H., "English Origins and New World Development: The Case of the Covenanted Militia in Seventeenth Century Massachusetts," *Past and Present,* 58 (1972), pp. 3-25.

Brodhead, James. *History of the State of New York.* Harper & Brothers, 1871.

Brooks, Lisa. *Our Beloved Kin: A New History of King Philip's War.* Yale University Press, 2019.

Buckner, Philip; and John Reid, eds. *The Atlantic Region to Confederation: A History.* University of Toronto Press, 1994.

Calloway, Colin Gordon. *After King Philip's War: Presence and Persistence in Indian New England.* Hanover, NH: University Press of New England, 1997.

Carr, J. Revell. *Seeds of Discontent: The Deep Roots of the American Revolution 1650–1750.* Walker & Company, 2008.

Chartrand, René . *Ticonderoga 1758: Montcalm's Victory Against All Odds.* Osprey, 2000.

_____. *Fort Frontenac 1758: Saving Face after Ticonderoga.* Osprey, 2001.

Church, Benjamin, as told to Thomas Church. *The History of Philip's War, Commonly Called The Great Indian War of 1675 and 1676.* Samuel G. Drake, ed. Exeter, NH: J & B Williams, 1829. Facsimile Reprint by Heritage Books, 1989.

Cubbison, Douglas. *The British Defeat of the French in Pennsylvania, 1758: A Military History of the Forbes Campaign Against Fort DuQuesne.* McFarland, 2010.

Danckaerts, Jasper. *Journal of Jasper Danckaerts.* B. B. James and J. F. Jameson, eds. New York: Scribner's, 1913.

Deforest, . L. E. *Captain John Underhill: Gentleman, Soldier of Fortune.* New York: Underhill Society of America, 1934.

Dodge, Edward J. *Relief is Greatly Wanted: the Battle of Fort William Henry.* Bowie, MD: Heritage Books, 1998.

Downame, John. *The Christian Warfare: Written Especially for Their Sakes who are Exercised in the Spirituall Conflict of Tentations, and are Afflicted in Conscience in the Sight Ande Sense of Their Sinnes* (1609).

_____. *The Christian Warfare Against the Deuill, World and Flesh...* W. Stansby,, ed. 2013.

Drake, Samuel A. *The Border Wars of New England, Commonly Called King William's and Queen Anne's Wars.* C. Scribner's Sons, 1897.

Fairchild, Byron. *Messrs. William Pepperrell: Merchants at Piscataqua.* Cornell University Press, 1954.

Folwell, Elizabeth, and Amy Godine, *Adirondack Odysseys.* Blue Mountain Lake, New York: The Adirondack Museum, 1997.

French, Allen. *The First Year of the American Revolution.* New York: Octagon, 1934.

Frothingham, R. *History of the Siege of Boston.* Little, Brown, 1903.

Gallagher, Edward J., "The" Wonder-Working Providence" as Spiritual Biography.," *Early American Literature,* 10.1 (1975), pp. 75-87.

General Laws of the Inhabitants of the Jurisdiction of New Plimouth. Plymouth: General Courts, 1685.

George E. Ellis. *The Red Man and the White Man.* Boston, 1882.

Gipson, Lawrence H. *The Great War for the Empire: The Years of Defeat, 1754–1757.* Knopf, 1946.
Greenough, C. P., "How Massachusetts Raised her Troops in the Revolution," *Collections of the Massachusetts Historical Society*, 55 (1921-22), pp. 345-70.
Grenier, John. *The First Way of War: American War Making on the Frontier.* Cambridge University Press. 2005.
_____. *The Far Reaches of Empire: War in Nova Scotia, 1710–1760.* Oklahoma University Press, 2008.
Griffith, William R. *The Battle of Lake George: England's First Triumph in the French and Indian War.* Charleston, SC: The History Press, 2016.
Haefeli, Evan; and Kevin Sweeney. *Captors and Captives: The 1704 French and Indian Raid on Deerfield.* University of Massachusetts Press, 2003.
Hall, David D. *Worlds of Wonder, Days of Judgment: Popular Religious Beliefs in Early New England.* Knopf, 1989.
Hall, Richard, "The Causes of the French and Indian War and the Origins of the 'Braddock Plan': Rival Colonies and Their Claims to the Disputed Ohio," in *Atlantic Politics, Military Strategy and the French and Indian War*: (2016), pp. 21–49.
Haller, William. *Rise of Puritanism; Or, the Way to the New Jerusalem as Set Forth in Pulpit and Press From Thomas Cartwright to John Lilburne and John Milton.* Harper & Row, 1957.
Harrison, Bird. *Navies in the Mountains: The Battles on the Waters of Lake Champlain and Lake George, 1609–1814.* Oxford University Press, 1962.
Holden, David. *Journal Kept by Sergeant David Holden of Groton, Massachusetts, during the Latter Part of the French and Indian War.* Cambridge, Ma,: Wilson & Son, 1889.
Hooker, Thomas. *A Survey of the Summe of Church Disciple.* London: Bellamy, 1648.
Hough, Franklin B. *General Gage's Informers.* University of Michigan Press, 1932.
_____. *The Day of Lexington and Concord, the 19th of April 1775.* Little Brown, 1925.
Hutchinson, Peter O., comp. *The Diary and Letters of His Excellency Thomas Hutchinson..* 2 vols. Boston: A. M. S., 1963.
James, Sydney V. *Colonial Rhode Island: A History.* Scribner's, 1975.
Johnson, Edward. *The Wonder-Working Providence of Sions Savior in New England.* London: Kyngston, 1654. J. F. Jameson, ed. (1910).
Kavenaugh, W. Keither, ed. *Foundations of Colonial America.* 3 vols. New York: Chelsea House, 1973.
Kawashima, Yasuhide. *Igniting King Philip's War: The John Sassamon Murder Trial.* University Press of Kansas, 2001.
Kidder, Frederick. *The Expeditions of Captain John Lovewell and His Encounters with the Indians.* Boston: Bartlett & Halliday, 1865.
Kimball, Everett. *The Public Life of Joseph Dudley.* New York: Harvard Historical Studies, 1911.
Leach, Douglas Edward. *Flintlock and Tomahawk: New England in King Philip's War* (1954). Parnassus Imprints reprint, 1992.
_____., ed. *A Rhode Islander Reports on King Philip's War.* Providence, R. I.:

Brown University Press 1963.

Lepore, Jill. *The Name of War: King Philip's War and the Origins of American Identity.* New York: Vintage Books, 1999.

Mahon, John K. *The American Militia: Decade of Decision, 1789–1800.* University of Florida Press, 1960.

_____. "Anglo-American Methods of Indian Warfare, 1676-1794," *Mississippi Valley Historical Review*, 15 [1958]: 254-75.

Mandell, Daniel R. *King Philip's War: Colonial Expansion, Native Resistance, and the End of Indian Sovereignty.* Johns Hopkins University Press, 2010.

Mason, Bernard, ed., *The American Colonial Crisis: The Daniel Leonard-John Adams Letters to the Press, 1774-1775.* Harper and Row, 1972.

Mason, John. *A Brief History of the Pequot War: Especially of the Memorable taking of their Fort at Mistick in Connecticut in 1637.* Boston: S. Kneeland & T. Green, 1736.

Mayo, Laurence S. *John Endecott.* New York: DaCapo, 1971.

Morton, Louis, "The Origins of American Military Policy," *Military Affairs,* 22 (1958), pp. 75-82.

Nester, William. *The Epic Battles of the Ticonderoga, 1758.* State University of New York Press, 2008.

O'Callaghan, Edmund Bailey, ed. *Documents Relative to the Colonial History of the State of New York.* 15 vols. State of New York, 1839-1883.

Osgood, Herbert Levi. *The American Colonies in the 17th Century.* 3 vols. Macmillan, 1907.

O'Sullivan, John; and Alan M. Meckler. *The Draft and Its Enemies: A Documentary History,* University of Illinois Press, 1974.

Oliver, Frederick Scott. *Alexander Hamilton.* New York: Crowell, 1970.

Palfrey, John G. *History of New England.* 4 vols. Boston, 1890.

Pargellis, Stanley, ed. *Military Affairs in North America, 1748-1756.* Hampden, Ct.: Anchor, 1969.

Parkman, Francis. *Half Century of conflict.* Little Brown, 1914.

_____. . *Montcalm and Wolfe.* 2 vols. Little, Brown, 1897.

Peckham, Howard H. *The Colonial Wars, 1698-1762.* University of Chicago Press, 1964.

Perry, David B. *Recollections of an Old Soldier.* Tarrytown, NY: W. Abbatt, 1928.

Peterson, Harold, "The Military Equipment of the Plymouth and Bay Colonies, 1620-1690," *New England Quarterly*, 20 (1947), pp. 197-208.

Peterson, Mark A. *The City-State of Boston: The Rise and Fall of an Atlantic Power, 1630–1865.* Princeton University Press. 2019.

Philbrick, Nathaniel. *Mayflower: A Story of Courage, Community, and War.* Penguin, 2006.

Pickering, Octavius. *The Life of Timothy Pickering.* 2 vols. Boston, 1867.

Pomeroy, Seth. *Journal and Papers of Seth Pomeroy, Sometime General in the Colonial Service.* New York: Society of Colonial Wars in the State of New York, 1926, publication number 38.

Poore, Benjamin P., ed. *The Federal and State Constitutions, Colonial Charters and Other Organic Laws of the United States.* 2 vols. U. S. Government Printing Office, 1877.

Powicke, Michael. *Military Obligation in Medieval England: A Study in Liberty and Duty.* Oxford: at the Clarendon Press, 1962.

Putnam, Rufus. *Journal of General Rufus Putnam Kept in Northern New York during Four Campaigns of the Old French and Indian War, 1757-1760.* Albany: Munsell, 1886.

Radabaugh, Jack S., "The Militia of Colonial Massachusetts," *Military Affairs,* 43 (1954), pp. 1-18.

Roberts, Oliver A. *History of the . . . Ancient and Honorable Artillery Company of Massachusetts, 1637-1888.* Boston: Mudge, 1895.

Row, Frank G. *The Indian and the Horse.* University of Oklahoma Press, 1955.

Russell, Peter, "Redcoats in the Wilderness: British Officers and Irregular Warfare in Europe and America, 1740 to 1760," *William and Mary Quarterly,* 35: 4 (1978) pp. 629–652.

Rutman, Darrell. "A Militant New World, 1607-1640." University of Virginia Ph. D. dissertation, 1959.

_____. *Winthrop's Boston.* University of North Carolina Press, 1965.

Schultz, Eric B.; and Michael J. Tougias. *King Philip's War: The History and Legacy of America's Forgotten Conflict.* W. W. Norton, 2000.

Schutz, J. A. *William Shirley, King's Governor of Massachusetts.* University of North Carolina, 1961.

Shannon, Timothy J. *Indians and Colonists at the Crossroads of Empire: The Albany Congress.* Cornell University Press, 2000.

Shurtleff, Nathaniel, ed. *Records of the Governor and Company of Massachusetts Bay in New England.* Nathaniel B. Shurtleff, ed. 5 vols. State of Massachusetts, 1854.

_____, ed. *The Compact with the Charters and Laws of the Colony of New Plymouth.* William Brigham, ed. State of Massachusetts, 1836.

_____, ed. *Records of the Colony of New Plymouth in New England.*

Shy, John. *Toward Lexington.* Princeton University Press, 1965.

Siebert, William H., "Loyalist Troops of New England," *New England Quarterly,* 4 (1931), pp. 108-47.

Slotkin, Richard; and James K. Folsom. *So Dreadful a Judgement: Puritan Responses to King Philip's War.* Weysleyan University Press, 1978.

Sosin, Jack. *English America and the Revolution of 1688: Royal Administration and the Structure of Provincial Government.* University of Nebraska Press, 1982.

Spencer, Henry Russell. *Constitutional Conflict in Provincial Massachusetts.* Columbus, Ohio: Heer, 1905.

Starbuck, David. *Massacre at Fort William Henry.* University Press of New England, 2002.

Steele, Ian K. *Betrayals: Fort William Henry & the 'Massacre'.* Oxford University Press, 1990.

Stevens, Benjamin F. *King Philip's War.* Boston: Sawyer, 1900.

Tomlinson, Everett T. *A Soldier of the Wilderness. A Story of Abercrombie's Defeat and the Fall of Fort Frontenac in 1758.* Chicago: W. A. Wilde Co., 1905.

Turney-High, Harry H. *Primitive War: Its Practice and Concepts.* University of South Carolina Press, 1949.

Upton, Emory. *Military Policy of the United States from 1775.* Washington; U. S. Government Printing Office, 1904

Vaughan, Alden T., ed. *Chronicles of the American Revolution.* Columbia University Press, 1965.

Waddell, Louis M.; and Bruce D. Bomberger. *The French and Indian War in Pennsylvania:Fortification and Struggle During the War for Empire.* Pennsylvania Historical and Museum Commission, 1996.

Waller, George. *Samuel Vetch, Colonial Enterpriser.* University of North Carolina Press, 1960.

Ward, Harry M. *Unite or Die: Intercolony Relations, 1690-1763.* Port Washington: Kennikat, 1971,

Weston, J. R. *The English Militia in the Eighteenth Century: The Story of a Political Issue, 1660–1802.* Routledge & Kegan Paul, 1965.

Whitmore, W. H., ed. *The Colonial Laws of Massachusetts reprinted from the Edition of 1660, with Supplements to 1672, Containing also the Body of Liberties of 1641.* Boston: State of Massachusetts, c.1860.

Williams, John; Stephen West; and John Taylor. *The Redeemed Captive Returning to Zion: or, The Captivity and Deliverance of Rev. John Williams of Deerfield. New York*: Kraus, 1969 reprint of a 1908 edition of Williams's narrative.

Winthrop, John. *History of New England.* James K. Hosmer, ed. 2 vols (1908).

_____. *Winthrop Papers.* 5 vols. Massachusetts Historical Society, 1929-47.

York, A. L. "The Myth of the Citizen-Soldier: Rhode Island Provincial Soldiers in the French and Indian War," Master thesis, U.S. Army Command and General Staff College, 2016.

Zelner, Kyle F. *A Rabble in Arms: Massachusetts Towns and Militiamen during King Philip's War.* New York University Press, 2009.

Made in the USA
Middletown, DE
11 December 2023